ELDERS *in*
CONGREGATIONAL
LIFE

ELDERS *in* CONGREGATIONAL LIFE

REDISCOVERING THE BIBLICAL MODEL
FOR CHURCH LEADERSHIP

PHIL A. NEWTON
FOREWORD BY MARK DEVER

Kregel
Academic & Professional

Elders in Congregational Life: Rediscovering the Biblical Model for Church Leadership

© 2005 by Phil A. Newton

Published by Kregel Publications, a division of Kregel, Inc., P.O. Box 2607, Grand Rapids, MI 49501.

Scripture taken from the *New American Standard Bible,* © Copyright 1960, 1962, 1963, 1968, 1971, 1972, 1973, 1975, 1977, 1995 by The Lockman Foundation. Used by permission.

Library of Congress Cataloging-in-Publication Data
Newton, Phil A..
Elders in congregational life: rediscovering the biblical model for church leadership / by Phil A. Newton.
    p. cm.
    Included bibliographical references and indexes.
    1. Elders (Church officers)—Baptists. 2. Baptists—Government. 3. Baptists—History. 4. Elders (Church officers)—Biblical teaching. I. Title.
BX6346.N48   2005
262'.146—dc22   2005006561

ISBN: 978-0-8254-3331-3

Printed in the United States of America

12 13 14 15 16 / 10 9 8 7 6

For Karen,
in honor and celebration of
thirty years together!

Contents

Foreword

The church is a reflection of God's Son. That's why leadership of the church is of utmost importance. The church is how the great hope—eternity with God in Christ—is to be seen. In the time between Christ's ascension and His return, Christians in covenant with one another—loving and caring, encouraging and sharing, correcting and bearing over the years—present the clearest picture of God's love that this world can see.

The Lord's church, His bride, is comprised of not merely a list of individuals who are redeemed and being sanctified. Rather, in the society of the saints is something that seems more human than in the life outside of it. And its radiance should shine out of our life together.

That was the plan from the beginning. From eternity past, God enjoyed full fellowship with Himself—Father, Son, and Holy Spirit. In the fullness of His love, He made this world, and then came Himself to redeem it. Those redeemed from the mass of this fallen world are ultimately to be with God forever.[1] In that great assembly, our union with Christ will know new depth, richness, and permanence. It will sparkle and shine, it will irradiate and warm, it will add passion and understanding that we can scarcely dream of now.

When speaking of leadership of the church—that is, the local church—is it any wonder, then, that *who should lead the church and how* is so critical? Phil Newton is the right man to write on this subject. He is a humble and joyful Christian who knows what it means to be united with Christ. More than that, he has decades of practice in leadership as a husband and father, and as a pastor of his own local church in Memphis. His understanding of God's Word is even deeper than his voice—a considerable statement, if you've ever talked with Phil or heard him preach! He's lived out the experience of leading a church as a single elder-pastor, and leading it through the transition to elder plurality. I, too, am a pastor who has led a church and lived through such a transition. For that reason, I salute Phil and commend his work to you.

Perhaps you have questions about leadership. Perhaps you're a deacon and you're worried about the ideas your pastor has been sharing. Maybe you're a member of many years, and you wonder how you should think about your church's structure. Perhaps you're a pastor, and through study of Scripture, or your own experience, or from watching other churches, you question the way your church is being led. You'll find help in this book, where biblical wisdom and pastoral warmth meet and give you the help you need. The answers and suggestions offered come with plenty of biblical and personal examples.

While many objections to having elders in a church can be imagined, this book addresses three superbly.

Is it Baptist? You might be thinking that this whole idea of having elders just "isn't Baptist!" When our church was considering the change, an older member said that very thing to me in front of a large Sunday school class.[2] If you share that concern, Phil's first chapter should be of interest to you. It looks at Baptists in history—in both England and America—and in particular at the question of having multiple elders in one local church. Phil cites primary sources to show that Baptists from their earliest times have acknowledged that pastors are elders (in that sense, Baptists have always had elders) and that Baptists have frequently preached, taught, and written in favor of having multiple elders in one local congregation. So, while it's true that other groups—Presbyterians, Dutch Reformed, Bible churches, Churches of Christ, and so on—have advocated having elders, Baptists, too, have so believed and taught. While it has certainly become a minority position among Baptists—and Phil even investigates this interesting fact—it has always been present, and today seems to be undergoing a renaissance. After reading this book, you'll see that having elders, indeed, "is Baptist."

Is it biblical? Others reading this book couldn't care less about whether eldership is Baptist. Perhaps you're in an Evangelical Free church, an independent church, or some other church, and you're in the process of reconsidering your structure. For you, the abiding concern is not one of denominational identity, but of biblical faithfulness. That's really the concern of the best Baptists—and the best Presbyterians, Methodists, Congregationalists, Episcopalians, and Lutherans as well! Christians understand the Bible to be God's revelation of Himself and His will for us, and as such, the Bible is the touchstone for our faith and practice. The Bible is how we learn to approach God both individually and in our churches. The Bible tells us how to run our lives, and the Bible tells us how God's church is to be ordered. So if you're concerned if eldership is biblical, you'll find this book a great help.

Elders in Congregational Life is full of careful, balanced, informed consideration of Scripture. Chapter 2 surveys the evidence in the New Testament, looking at the various titles that are used for church leaders and addressing the question of multiple elders in a single congregation. Chapter 3 considers the examples in the book of Acts. The whole of part 2 focuses on three central texts—Acts 20, the record of Paul's meeting with the Ephesian elders; Hebrews 13, the words to the leaders of congregations; and 1 Peter 5, Peter's words about being an undershepherd of God's flock. In all three parts, Scripture is regularly both referred and deferred to. Phil not only knows the Bible but he intends to obey it. As a pastor himself, he has gone through the difficulties of leading a congregation to change. Why would he do that? He did it because of his belief in the sufficiency of Scripture, and his commitment to be ruled by it, both in how he approaches God and in how he leads his church to do the same. After reading this book, you'll come to agree with Phil, and you'll see that having elders is, in fact, biblical.

Is it best? Finally, your concern may be a more practical one. You may be concerned not so much about your denominational identity, or the deep debates on specific texts of the Bible. Perhaps you think that having a plurality of elders does seem the most biblical way to lead a church, but you wonder, *Is it really best?* Is it the best thing for your church at this time? How would you go about it? Perhaps your pastor is promoting the idea right now. Maybe he gave you this book to read. (Don't you love the way pastors give you books to read, like you don't have anything else to do?) Maybe you're part of a church leadership team studying together on this subject. Maybe you're a pastor who's convinced of having elders in your church, but have no idea of how you would actually do it. Take heart, my friends, you've found the right book!

I know of no other book that gives such particular and practical consideration for transitioning to plural elders. The whole of part 3, "From Theory to Practice," is a wonderfully practical guide for evaluating elders, presenting them, and beginning to have them function in your church. By the wealth of information in these chapters, it's obvious that Phil has lived through the process, and he's willing to share his own experiences—good and bad—in order to help us have even better experiences in our churches. If you read this book, you'll see that having elders is, without doubt, the best way to lead your church.

One more word of testimony: I'm enthusiastic about this book because I'm excited about what having elders has meant to me as a senior pastor. Since 1994 I've had the privilege of serving Capitol Hill Baptist Church in Washington, D.C. This church, founded in 1878, had grown large in the early part of the twentieth century, but declined in number during the last half of the century. In the early months and years of my stewardship of this very traditional (and senior) Baptist congregation, I openly taught on having elders—and I didn't mean just more staff members. I meant understanding that Christ gives His church teachers, some of whom may be financially supported by the church, others who are not. I was convinced that it was consistent with Baptist history, that it was biblical, and that it was simply best that we move to having a plurality of elders.

These elders, I taught, would help me guide the flock. I taught from 1 Timothy and Titus, from 1 Peter and from Acts 20, from Hebrews 13 and Ephesians 4. When I had opportunity, I instructed the congregation. I used John MacArthur's booklet on elders,[3] circulating multiple copies of it in the congregation. We had the privilege of D. A. Carson coming to our church, and teaching on this very topic. I cited the example of other well-known Baptist pastors—from C. H. Spurgeon to John Piper—who had elders.

Finally, after two years of careful, committee-filled consideration, the congregation voted to adopt a new constitution with the plurality of elders. Only one member voted against it; at this writing six years later, he's still a happy member of the church in regular attendance. What has been the result? Six years of improved pastoral care, wisdom in decision-making, help in difficulties, and joy for me as I've seen mature, godly men give sacrificially of their time and lives to lead the congregation that God has given them. It's been a wonderful time.

As you read this book, I pray that God will make it useful to you, and that you will experience as did I the goodness and care of God through the order that He has established for His church. If God has deliberately instructed us, let us give ourselves to hear and heed His word on every point—even down to having elders recognized in the church.

Authority is a good gift of God to us. In both exercising and submitting to authority, we come to know God better. And especially because this gift of authority is so little understood and so often misused in our churches, I pray that through this book God will help you and your church.

MARK DEVER
Capitol Hill Baptist Church
Washington, D.C.

Acknowledgments

The Lord has made me a debtor. In writing *Elders in Congregational Life,* I owe much to many. My own congregation, the South Woods Baptist Church in Memphis, has walked with me during the long journey of this book, giving much encouragement and prayer. My fellow elders, Jim Carnes, Tommy Campbell, and Tom Tollett, shaped much of the book's contents by their faithful examples and insightful discussions. Their extended dialogues on the details of elder plurality, coupled with Tom's special editorial precision, have added to the book's usefulness. Suzanne Buchanan, wife of one of our deacons and former law journal editor, provided remarkable aid. Her red ink translated into welcomed changes. Richard and Ginger Hamlet gave me a quiet office during a two-week sabbatical so that I might write without interruption. Several friends, including Mark Dever, Ray Pritchard, Danny Akin, the late Stephen Olford, David Olford, Tom Ascol, Matt McCullough, and Randy McClendon, applied keen eyes to the rough draft, offering invaluable suggestions. Besides graciously penning the book's foreword, Mark paved the way for this book by his writing and speaking on the subject of elders. Ray's lifelong friendship and encouragement in writing has helped me more times than I can number. The Olfords initiated my teaching on the subject, which provided an international laboratory for discussing elder plurality with Christian leaders across the globe. My friend and colleague in pastoral ministry, Todd Wilson, held the reins quite often while I wrote, and came to my aid on numerous occasions for both research and answers to my computer questions. Jim Weaver, Steve Barclift, and the staff of Kregel Publications have shown great patience and skill in the coaching and editing process. I am especially grateful to my wife, Karen, for her support, encouragement, and listening ear as I sounded out many ideas over the past few years in contemplating and writing this book. She is an incomparable partner in life and ministry. The rest of the family—Kelly, Adam, Addie, Andrew, John, Lizzy, Stephen, and Mama Jane—have added their support as well!

My love and affection for the great Shepherd of the sheep has grown as I've studied His wise design for the church. May He be glorified by this contribution to His flock.

Introduction

"Why elders?" The question was posed to me as our congregation journeyed through the transition to elder leadership. My home church did not have elders; neither did the three churches where I had previously served as pastor. Although elders could be found among Presbyterian and Church of Christ congregations in the community, Baptists just did not have elders. So why should I spend the energy and time, not to mention stir up potential trouble, to move to a leadership structure of plural eldership?

Three primary elements moved me into the direction of a plurality of elders: Scripture, Baptist history, and practical issues of church life. While delivering sermons that dealt with biblical texts teaching elder plurality, I experienced numerous uncomfortable moments—uncomfortable because I softened or ignored the teaching due to my own pastoral context. References to elders abound throughout the New Testament, so it is impossible to not encounter these texts while preaching consecutively through books of the Bible. I adopted the superficial explanation that equated the early church elders with today's pastoral staffs. This satisfied my audience but it was clear to me that I imposed a modern perspective on the ancient text. Before continuing to offer this explanation to my congregation, I had to be sure that this common interpretation was true to the biblical text. If, through studying the Scripture myself, I was not convinced that this interpretation was biblical, how could I convince my congregation? The more I studied the biblical texts, the less support I found for simply equating elders with the modern church staff. Biblical integrity called for a change in the way that I addressed these texts.

History played a vital role in affecting my thought as well. When I was a teenager, I discovered that my home church recognized elders in its early history. The first few pastors were identified as Elder Gibson, Elder Hudson, and Elder Jennings. Why were they called *elder* in the nineteenth century if, indeed, they were pastors? The answer to that question came many years later when a friend with a Ph.D. in Church History from the Southwestern Baptist Theological Seminary sent to me a copy of W. B. Johnson's address, "The Rulers of a Church of Christ" from his *The Gospel Developed Through the Government and Order of the Churches of Jesus Christ* (1846). Johnson, the first president of the Southern Baptist Convention, clearly set forth the biblical and practical necessity for a plurality of elders in Baptist life. Johnson's notoriety as a leader among early Southern Baptists made his address no small historical marker for elders in congregational life. If the congregational life of some, or perhaps even many, eighteenth- and nineteenth-century Baptists included the practice of elder leadership, then why did Baptists in the nineteenth and twentieth centuries transition to a leadership structure of a single pastor, staff, and deacons?

Lastly, practical concerns gave much reason for questioning the common authority structure in Baptist churches. I had experienced my share of church conflicts, disheartening business meetings, poorly qualified deacons, and power struggles in congregational life. I witnessed firsthand the discontinuity between pastor and deacons that affected the unity and viability of a church. Was this just the way things had to be if you were a Baptist? Many thought so. I read, too, another pastor's newsletter article that likened Baptists to fighting alley cats: "So don't try to change us," he stated. But God's Word would not allow me to be resigned to such assertions. How would I answer the Lord of the church if I acquiesced to conflict and confusion in church leadership?

Knowing my accountability to the Lord for the way that I led the church I served, I also knew that I had to take a higher road—even if the price were also high. Is there a better way—a more biblical way—to conduct church life? That's the question that I faced in the late 1980s, and one that many are currently facing. The necessity for change must not be ignored, but the methodology need not cause knee-jerk reactions that upset the equilibrium of congregations. Church leaders and congregations must labor, however, to discover God's revealed will in the Scriptures and, then, faithfully obey it.

Elders in Congregational Life does not exhaust the subject of elder leadership. Rather, it explores Scripture and church history, and then offers some workable recommendations for pastors and church leaders interested in transitioning to elder leadership. Part 1 addresses the question, "Why do we need plural elders in church life?" It explores the history of elders among Baptists and considers implications drawn from early Baptist confessional documents. Although this book is written from the perspective of my own denomination, churches from other congregational settings may identify as well. Familiarity with church history helps to flesh out the applications of Scripture in any ministry. Following the historical study, a biblical and theological investigation establishes the framework for plural eldership.

Part 2 addresses the pastoral role, expounding three different texts that address elders and spiritual leadership. Rather than looking at broad theological matters as in part 1, part 2 isolates particular texts in order to delineate the basic biblical framework for elder plurality and demonstrate how that framework can be studied in a congregational setting. Thus, the purpose of part 2 is twofold: first, to further explore the meaning of *elder* in the New Testament context; second, to offer a model for biblical expositions that might prove helpful to pastors and leaders in teaching their own congregations. Congregations are more likely to follow leadership changes when convinced that Scripture demands the change. Preaching through the various passages addressing local church leadership provides the context for swallowing traditions and following God's will.

Part 3 addresses some of the questions and perplexities of transitioning to elder plurality. It offers recommendations for laying groundwork for eventual transition to elder leadership, and for trusting the Great Shepherd to apply what is needed in your own setting.

PART ONE

Why Elders?

CHAPTER ONE

Why *Baptist Elders* Is Not an Oxymoron

Old photos of old men raised questions in my young mind. As a teenager, my curiosity was piqued upon seeing portraits of the pastors who had served my home church during the nineteenth century. Each bore the caption *Elder* under his name. I knew that elders served in the local Presbyterian and Church of Christ congregations, but I had never heard of an elder in a one-hundred-year-old Baptist church. Yet the old pictures were not lying—the First Baptist Church of Russellville, Alabama, had once recognized elders. It appears that presbyters—plural eldership—from congregations in neighboring towns held the responsibility for establishing and maintaining new churches in the area. First Baptist of Russellville was founded in 1867 "with Elders R. J. Jennings and Mike Finney constituting the presbytery."[1]

True, in some circles the title *Elder* was once used much the same way that *Pastor* or *Brother* is used today, yet beyond the title, the *practice* of plural eldership existed among some of the churches. Baptist historian Greg Wills, while addressing the egalitarian distinction of Baptists' functioning democratically, points out that in previous centuries "government [as distinguished from matters of discipline] related to the election of church officers—deacons, elders, and pastors." He further explains, "Antebellum Baptists frequently referred to ordained ministers as *elders*. Some churches also appointed 'ruling' elders, who were not ordained ministers."[2] In detailing the history of early Baptists of Tennessee, J. H. Grimes frequently refers to pastors as *elder*. He identifies Elder John Bond in Statesville as "only a licensed minister at this time, but was regularly ordained by Union Church A.D. 1820, by a presbytery consisting of Elders Joshua Lester and David Gordon."[3] Bond subsequently served as pastor, but was called *elder* even before assuming the pastorate. Within Tennessee Baptist churches, Grimes further identifies plural eldership of men involved in pastoral leadership but not drawing a salary as "lay elders."[4]

ELDER PLURALITY AMONG AMERICAN BAPTISTS

David Tinsley—a prominent Baptist serving in Georgia in the late eighteenth century alongside Jesse Mercer's father, Silas Mercer—was ordained four times: "The first was to the office of a deacon, the second to that of a ruling elder, his third ordination was to the office of preaching the gospel, and in the fourth place he was ordained an evangelist by Col. Samuel Harris, while he officiated in the dignified character of the Apostle of Virginia."[5] The first two of these offices represented nonpaid, non-staff positions in the local church, placing Tinsley as part of the plural eldership in his church. His service with the noted leader Silas Mercer demonstrates the prominence given to plural eldership among Baptists.[6]

Minutes of the Philadelphia Baptist Association 1707–1807—notably the leading association of Baptists in the Colonial period—gives ample evidence of plural eldership. In 1738, a question before the association sought to determine whether a ruling elder who had been set apart by the laying on of hands and "should afterward be called by the church, by reason of his gifts, to the word and doctrine [i.e., as pastor], must be again ordained by imposition of hands." The answer was simple: "Resolved in the affirmative."[7] A cursory reading of the *Minutes* clearly demonstrates the commonality of plural eldership among eighteenth-century Baptists in the Northeast. Recognizing a distinction between ruling elders and those ministering the Word appears to have been the norm in the Philadelphia Association; ordination of ruling elders was left to the discretion of the individual churches.[8] Plurality was clearly their practice.

In the South, some Baptist churches of the eighteenth and nineteenth centuries practiced plural eldership. "It was sometimes a formal recognition of the ordained ministers, the elders of their membership," writes Wills. "These elders assisted the pastor as necessary in preaching and administering baptism and the Lord's Supper. They were leaders of the congregation by their wisdom, piety, knowledge, and experience. Such churches recognized the gifts and calling of all elders among them."[9]

It is found at this point that many Baptists made a distinction between "ruling elders" and "teaching elders." Ruling elders focused on the administrative and governing issues of church life, while the teaching elders exercised pastoral responsibilities, including administering the ordinances. By 1820 the title *ruling elders* had actively faded in Baptist church life, ecclesiastical authority coming to reside in the congregation. Some then considered that the pastor and deacons constituted the eldership. Not all agreed, including the first president of the Southern Baptist Convention, W. B. Johnson, who "taught that Christ strictly required each church to have plural eldership," which implied a distinction between plural eldership and plural diaconate.[10]

ENGLISH BAPTISTS

The practice of including elders in Baptist life did not begin in America. Plural eldership was common in England during the seventeenth and eighteenth centuries. A. C. Underwood offers several examples of lay elders[11] who were part of the plurality of elders in local English Baptist churches. He notes that early Baptists not only recognized elder plurality, but also distinguished the functions of elders within local churches. He mentions the seventeenth-century Broadmead Church in Bristol, which had a pastor, ruling elders, deacons, and deaconesses (who were presumably widows supported by the largesse of a ruling elder).[12]

In England, Baptist eldership differed from Presbyterian eldership. Early Baptists "recoiled at the prospect" of elders in one church functioning as elders in another. Hence the idea of a synod or presbytery outside of the local church would be unheard of among them because of the congregational perspective concerning the weight of authority placed in the local church. The only exception appears to be when elders helped in ordaining officers or administering the ordinances upon approval of the local church. These functioned as ministers of the gospel, but without pastoral authority in the local church.[13]

Unlike Presbyterians, most of the English Baptists of this era rejected the idea of "ruling elders." The Devonshire Square Church in London, where William Kiffin was pastor, recognized "a parity within the eldership," that is, each elder shared responsibility and authority within the church. Quoting from primary sources, James Renihan notes, "At Kensworth, Bedfordshire, in 1688, three men were chosen jointly and equally to offitiate [sic] in the room of [the deceased pastor] Brother Hayward in breaking bread, and other administration of ordinances, and the church did at the same time agree to provide and mainetane [sic] all at there [sic] one charge."[14] The renowned Benjamin Keach rejected the idea of ruling elders as a distinct position, but allowed that the church might "choose some able and discreet Brethren to be *Helps* in *Government*," presumably either as a separate alliance or more likely as members of plural eldership.[15] Renihan points out "that at least a small number of the churches made a distinction between teaching and ruling elders." In such cases, "The pastor was the chiefe [sic] of ye Elders of ye Church," while the ruling elders shared with him its oversight.[16] Certainly not all of the English Baptist churches of this era followed elder plurality but "the majority of the Particular Baptists were committed to a plurality and parity of elders in their churches," believing plural eldership "necessary for a completed church."[17]

Elders were never to lord their position over their churches. They were "stewards responsible to their Master, and servants to their people." Their duties, according to Nehemiah Coxe in a 1681 ordination sermon, were "prayer (leading worship), preaching and the exercise of discipline; and the private duties as visiting the flock, encouraging, exhorting and rebuking them."[18] Hanserd Knollys, another of the remarkable leaders among English Baptists of the seventeenth century, described the duties of plural eldership:

> The Office of a *Pastor, Bishop,* and *Presbyter,* or *Elder* in the Church of God, is to take the Charge, Oversight, and Care of

those Souls in which the Lord Jesus Christ hath committed to
them, to feed the Flock of God; to watch for their Souls, to Rule,
Guide and Govern them . . . according to the laws, Constitutions
and ordinances of the Gospel.[19]

Confessional documents and statements on church polity among early
Baptists in England and the United States substantiate the practice of
plural eldership. The London Confession of 1644 affirmed,

That being thus joyned [sic], every Church has power given them
from Christ for their better well-being, to choose to themselves
meet persons into the office of Pastors, Teachers, Elders, Deacons, being qualified according to the Word, as those which Christ
has appointed in his Testament, for the feeding, governing, serving, and building up of his Church, and that none other have
power to impose them, either these or any other.[20]

Similar to the London Confession of Baptists, the 1658 Savoy Declaration—the Congregationalist confession that contained much of the
substance of later Baptist confessions—identifies "Pastors, Teachers, Elders, and Deacons" as "the officers appointed by Christ to be chosen and
set apart by the church."[21] The Baptist Confession of 1688 (the Philadelphia Confession) follows the language of the Savoy Declaration with a
change only in the offices identified as "bishops or elders and deacons."[22]
The New Hampshire Confession of 1833—the foundational document
for Southern Baptist's 1925 *Baptist Faith and Message*—identifies the local church's only scriptural officers as "Bishops, or Pastors, and Deacons,
whose qualifications, claims, and duties are defined in the epistles to
Timothy and Titus."[23] The Abstract of Principles (1858)—the confession still used at the Southern and Southeastern Baptist Theological Seminaries—stated, "The regular officers of a Church are Bishops or Elders,
and Deacons." Although the 1925 *Baptist Faith and Message* of Southern
Baptists identifies the office of elders, both the 1963 and 2000 *Baptist
Faith and Message* revisions eliminate the titles *bishop* and *elder*, opting
for "its Scriptural officers are pastors and deacons." The change demonstrates how plural eldership fell out of use in Baptist practice.[24]

True, the confessional statements are somewhat vague, allowing those affirming elder plurality and those objecting to it to fit into the confessional framework. Certainly not all of the English Baptist and Colonial Baptist churches practiced plural eldership. By some accounts, only a minority did so. Yet the presence of plural eldership among notable leaders and in strong churches contradicts the notion that eldership is an anomaly among Baptists.

Thus, modern Baptists seeking to embrace plural eldership have a viable heritage as a foundation.[25] This heritage radiates clearly through some of the polity documents of earlier Baptists. Benjamin Griffith, in "A Short Treatise Concerning a True and Orderly Gospel Church" (1743), clearly taught elder plurality, pointing to ruling elders as those gifted "to assist the pastor or teacher in the government of the church."[26] He further explained, "The works of teaching and ruling belong both to the pastor; but in case he be unable; or the work of ruling too great for him, God hath provided such for his assistance, and they are called ruling elders."[27] Griffith's concept was that such elders were to come alongside the pastor who labors at the ministry of the Word, strengthening his hands for the demands of Christian ministry. In this sense, Griffith insists on the practicality of employing a plurality of elders "in easing the pastor or teacher, and keeping up the honor of the ministry."[28]

W. B. JOHNSON AND SOUTHERN BAPTISTS

As one of the founders of the Southern Baptist Convention, and its first denominational president, W. B. Johnson left a legacy of biblical fidelity and passion for the gospel. His work on church polity, "The Gospel Developed through the Government and Order of the Churches of Jesus Christ" (1846), remains trustworthy in encouraging Baptist churches to faithfulness to the Word of God. After outlining the biblical evidence of plural eldership in the first century churches, Johnson explained that each elder (or "bishop" as he called them, although he preferred the term *overseer*) brought "a particular talent" to the needs of the church. He added, "The importance and necessity of a bishopric for each church, embodying gifts for various services, is thus most obvious for the accomplishment of one of the great ends for which Christ came into the world, and for which, when he ascended up on high, he received gifts for men" (i.e., the purpose of ministry as outlined in Eph. 4:12–16).[29] In a plurality, each elder brings a different set of gifts and abilities so that the whole body profits by this sharing together in ministry. Explaining the benefit of more minds thinking together upon the complexities of ministry, he states, "A plurality in the bishopric is of great importance for mutual counsel and aid, that the government and edification of the flock may be promoted in the best manner."[30] In reviewing the scriptural teaching on elders, Johnson explains, "These rulers were all equal in rank and authority, no one having a preeminence over the rest. This satisfactorily appears from the fact, that the same qualifications were required in all, so that though some labored in word and doctrine, and others did not, the distinction between them was not in rank, but in the character of their service."[31]

Johnson was realistic. While acknowledging that elder plurality was required, he noted that some churches might not be able immediately to establish a plurality: "In a church where more than one [elder] cannot be obtained, that one may be appointed upon the principle, that as soon as another can be procured there shall be a plurality."[32] Further, Johnson clearly distinguished between elders and deacons. The elders' office is spiritual, while that assigned to the deacons is temporal. "Whatever of temporal care the interests of the church require, *that* care falls upon the *deacons,* as the *servants* of the church."[33] Of course, deacons function in plurality as well.

May it be concluded, then, that every Baptist church of the past had elder plurality? Obviously not. In light, however, of Baptists' historical emphasis on the autonomy of the local church, clearly the Baptists noted believed plurality of elders to be the New Testament model. After surveying historical Baptist confessions, John Piper drew his own conclusion: "The least we can say from this historical survey of Baptist Confessions is that *it is false to say that the eldership is unbaptistic. On the contrary, the eldership is more baptistic than its absence, and its disappearance is a modern phenomenon that parallels other developments in doctrine that make its disappearance questionable at best.*"[34]

RECENT DEMISE IN ELDER PLURALITY

The past two hundred years have witnessed the demise in elder plurality among Baptists. Pastors are expected to abandon the shepherding role for that of becoming "ranchers," a term used often by church growth leaders. Many well-known pastors resemble corporate CEOs rather than the New Testament office of humble shepherd. Their staffs, too, have taken on the corporate board air. Churches have become big businesses, requiring corporate structures that mirror many successful companies. Some of the megachurch pastors have achieved such success that they now, in fact, advise businesses.

A candid look at polity in churches at large today raises questions regarding our diligence to conform to Scripture. Are our churches more conformed to the image of Christ? Are we so transformed by holiness of life that we are the salt and light in our communities that our Lord declared us to be? Are the moral and family values of church members appreciably different from the typical American home? Are local congregations nurtured and disciplined as were our New Testament counterparts? Are the inflated membership rolls that have been fomented by the success-driven, CEO model for the church legitimate bragging rights in denominational circles? Does the average church display the kind of unity that the apostles exhorted and for which Jesus Christ prayed? Do church staffs make the most of the godly, capable leaders within their congregation? Are pastors and staff members held accountable to anyone besides themselves? Could it be that the alarming rate of immoral behavior among ministers is due to a disconnection between the church staff and a plurality of godly elders comprised of staff and lay leadership?

Baptist forebears sought to anchor their church structure and practice in the teaching of Holy Scripture. Shunning conformity to the world's designs that were prevalent in their times, these stalwarts used the truths of Scripture to forge a path for their heirs. In the end, whether or not Baptists historically practiced plural eldership is secondary. The primary focus for church leaders today must be to understand the teaching of God's Word, and then to order the local church accordingly. History merely serves to affirm the veracity of Scripture.

REFLECTIONS

- What part does history play in one's understanding of modern church life?
- Did all of the early Baptist churches practice elder plurality?
- What was W. B. Johnson's position on plural eldership?
- Why was there a movement away from elder plurality among nineteenth- and twentieth-century Baptists?

CHAPTER TWO

Elders in the New Testament

The danger facing modern congregations is to read into the Scriptures a twenty-first-century concept of church government. We have added plenty of "bells and whistles": church staff positions for preaching, mass media, recreation, committees for every imaginable need, corporate structure rivaling "Fortune 500" companies, and seminars that show every church "how to do it." This drive to increase growth and expand ministry has complicated the church's structure. The consequences have been twofold: ministry, with both its privileges and burdens, has shifted to the "professional" staff, while bypassing gifted leaders whom God has already placed within the ranks of membership; and nurturing, equipping, and discipling believers to be salt and light in the world gets lost in the shuffle of big events and choreographed performances. Both the church and a spiritually needy world suffer as a result. That is why understanding the biblical basis for elders is crucial in establishing vibrant, Christ-centered churches.[1]

No single text in the New Testament sets forth all the details necessary for structuring a local church. But by combining the various texts addressing leadership, structure, and decision making, a framework for church life can be constructed. The framework may be fleshed out in different ways—depending on cultural influences, personalities, pressing needs, and gifts within the church. Nevertheless, several elements are essential to every local church.

Even during the days of the apostles and prophets, the New Testament church had developed a structure that included the offices of elder and deacon. This pattern has been affirmed in the evangelical confessions, with elders primarily addressing the spiritual needs and deacons addressing the temporal needs of their congregations.

THREE TITLES

Elder (Presbuteros)

The title *elder* can be found throughout the New Testament. In the two-dozen cases of usage of *elder* (Greek, *presbuteros*) in the Gospels, most refer to those men who, by reason of age and status, were involved in the Jewish community's leadership structure. Generally, the Gospels do not portray these particular elders favorably since they joined the spiritual leaders of the Jewish community in rejecting the Messiah (e.g., Matt. 15:2; 16:21; 21:23; Mark 8:31; Luke 22:52). Elsewhere in the Gospels, the word simply conveys greater age (John 8:9).[2]

In the New Testament Christian community, elders functioned as representatives of the church. Christian elders in Jerusalem, for example, received from Barnabas and Saul relief gifts on behalf of believers in Antioch (Acts 11:30). Afterward, when Paul and Barnabas circled back to the churches they had established during their first missionary journey, they "appointed elders for them in every church" (14:23). Multiple elders were set apart in each of the infant churches of Asia Minor so that they might be nurtured and protected—clearly establishing the pattern of plural eldership. The authority of these first Christian elders came not by virtue of age or length of membership in the church, but by way of the weightiness of the ministry they had received from the apostolic missionaries.[3] When those missionaries departed, the work of preaching the gospel, strengthening the disciples, and encouraging them in the face of tribulations belonged to the elders (vv. 21–22).

It would not, in fact, have been surprising had Luke stopped everything in the process of writing Acts to announce the development of elders! Just as Luke assumed (and never commanded) the work of planting new churches, likewise he assumed (but never commanded) the appointment of elders. The historical record clearly demonstrates the normative practices of the New Testament church—and plural eldership was at the heart of these practices. The balance of the book of Acts gives evidence that elders were part of the early churches' leadership structure.

Although the structure evolved slowly in the early years, plural eldership was part-and-parcel of church life. Elders joined the apostles in receiving Paul and Barnabas along with report of their missionary endeavors (15:2, 4). The elders stood with the apostles in addressing the problem of Judaizers who attempted to subvert young converts with their legalism (v. 22). A letter drafted for the new churches was sent from both the apostles and the elders, demonstrating the unique authority given to these representatives of the Jerusalem church (v. 23). Elders' authority in doctrinal issues became clear as Paul passed along this decree on his second missionary journey (16:4). On his third missionary journey, while in Miletus, Paul met with the elders of the church at Ephesus for a final exhortation before his long ordeal of Roman imprisonment (20:17).

The unusual thing, then, about elders in the early church is that they were not unusual. Every example shows them in plurality as they served individual churches in the early years of Christianity (except where a particular elder or overseer is mentioned, e.g., 1 Peter 5:1; 2 John 1; 3 John 1).

Overseer (Episkopos)

Coupled with elders are both *overseers* (bishops) and *pastors*. The *overseer* (Greek, *episkopos*), like plural elders, was common during the early church times. The Greeks used the term to define an office that had superintending functions, whether in political or religious circles.[4] It conveyed the idea of "to look upon, to consider, to have regard to, something or someone." Hence it implied caring for or watching over others, particularly those in need.[5] Fourth and fifth century B.C. Athens used *episkopoi* as a title for state officials who acted as supervisors in maintaining public order, often by exercising judicial powers.[6]

The Epistles use *overseer* or *bishop* interchangeably with *elder*. Paul, during his ministry in Crete, instructs Titus to "appoint elders in every city" (again note the plurality of elders in the single churches in the small cities of Crete). The apostle then expands upon the qualifications of elders, calling them overseers (Titus 1:5–7). Paul specifically addresses his letter to the overseers and deacons in Philippi (Phil. 1:1). In 1 Timothy 3:1–7, Paul gives qualifications for elders, which are similar to the qualifications given to Titus for overseers (1 Tim. 3:1–7). Peter used the verbal form of overseeing *(episkopeō)* as he explained the duties of elders (1 Peter 5:1–3). Luke also used both the terms *elder* and *overseer* to describe the office and function of the Ephesian elders (Acts 20:17, 28). All of these passages assume the establishment of overseers in church leadership. Elders prove, then, to be essential to the early church's leadership and ongoing stability.

The type of leadership overseers are to provide must mirror that of Christ, whom Peter described as "the Shepherd and Guardian *[episkopon]* of your souls" (1 Peter 2:25). Peter uses the term *overseer* to speak of the sufficiency of Christ's death on the cross so that believers might "live to righteousness" (v. 24). It is through the gospel that believers are now delivered from "continually straying like sheep" (v. 25). Christ is called the "Guardian of your souls," which implies that He watches over those who are His own in order to preserve them from the effects of sin and to direct them into lives of righteousness. Thus, like Christ, an overseer will watch over the spiritual lives of those under his charge, seeking to protect them from the perils of false teaching and deceit of sin, so that the church might live as salt and light to the glory of Christ.

Pastor (Poimēn)

Although the term *pastor (poimēn)* was translated only once in its noun form, the title joins those of *elder* and *overseer* in deepening the hues of this church office (Eph. 4:11). The word literally means "shepherd," and is translated thus throughout the Gospels and in two of the Epistles (e.g., Matt 9:36; 25:32; 26:31; John 10:2, 11–12, 16; Heb. 13:20; 1 Peter 2:25, with most referring to Christ as the Shepherd of His flock). It served as a common epithet among rulers of the ancient east.[7] Both Psalm 23 and the Good Shepherd motif in John 10 provide rich meaning to the shepherd leading, restoring, guiding, protecting, and providing for the sheep, and calling the sheep by name, laying down his life for the sheep, and knowing the sheep intimately. When listing the ascension gifts to the church, Paul couples the terms *pastor* and *teacher* in Ephesians 4:11, and is better translated, "teaching shepherds" or "pastor-teachers." The nature of the term indicates protecting, governing, guiding, nurturing, and caring for the flock.[8] Christ used the verbal form *(poimainō)* in His postresurrection charge to Peter: "shepherd My sheep" (John 21:16). The verb also joins *elder* and *overseer* in explaining the function of elders to shepherd God's flock (Acts 20:28; 1 Peter 5:2). Paul also uses it metaphorically when describing the work that he and Barnabas did among the Corinthians (1 Cor. 9:7).

Elder—the spiritual maturity of the office
Overseer—leadership and direction for the church
Pastor—feeding, nurturing, and protecting the flock

While *elder* appears to be the dominant term for the church office dealing with the spiritual needs of the local church, *overseer* and *pastor*, as has been noted, are used synonymously with elder. Each provides a clearer picture of the dignity and function of elders in church life: *elder* emphasizes the spiritual maturity required for this office; *overseer* implies the leadership and direction given to the church; *pastor* suggests feeding, nurturing, and protecting the flock. The diverse cultural background in each New Testament church may have determined which title was applied to this plurality of godly leaders. Although it may not be possible to make a clear-cut distinction, it seems that the Jewish Christians preferred *elder*, while the Gentile Christians more often used the title *overseer*, each referring to the same office. The only use of the noun *pastor* is found in Ephesians, yet it can be surmised that each of the churches found this title to be helpful in describing the function of their spiritual leaders.

PLURAL LEADERSHIP

It is difficult to build a scriptural argument against elder plurality in the early church. Bill Murray points out, "Both the churches at Philippi and Ephesus are said to have multiple 'elders.' These cannot be 'pastors of several churches' in the areas of Philippi or Ephesus." And he explains why. "First, each church is mentioned singularly. Second, elders *[plural]* are mentioned." Then he deduces, "multiple elders at EACH church."[9] Added to this, unless a particular elder is addressed, the term—along with *overseer* and *pastor*—is always used in the plural (e.g., Acts 11:30; 14:23; 15:2, 4, 22–23; 16:4; 20:17, 28; Eph. 4:12; 1 Tim. 5:17; Titus 1:5; James 5:14; 1 Peter 5:1). Wayne Grudem surveys the New Testament texts on elders and draws clear conclusions:

> First, no passage suggests that any church, no matter how small, had only one elder. The consistent New Testament pattern is a plurality of elders "in every church" (Acts 14:23) and "in every city" (Titus 1:5). Second, we do not see a diversity of forms of government in the New Testament church, but a unified and consistent pattern in which every church had elders governing it and keeping watch over it (Acts 20:28; Heb. 13:17; 1 Peter 5:2–3).[10]

Who were the elders in the early church? In the modern counterpart of senior pastor and church staff, we can easily read our common practice into the New Testament pattern. Without seminaries or Bible institutes to produce "pastors," the early church selected men from within their membership to serve as elders. When Paul and Barnabas returned to Lystra, Iconium, and Antioch, "they . . . appointed elders for them in every church" (Acts 14:23). It is of note that the appointees were not ministerial apprentices or even seasoned pastors. Rather, Paul and Barnabas chose men in plurality from within each of the churches to serve as elders in their own congregations. We have no evidence that the office of elder evolved into a function comparable to modern full-time ministry service. Accordingly, we may conclude that godly men from within the church—men that demonstrated Christian character and leadership qualities—were set apart to serve their churches while continuing with their normal occupations. While some of these men might have had preaching gifts, certainly all of them were "able to teach" (1 Tim. 3:2).

Titus followed this same model of appointing elders while acting as the apostolic representative on the island of Crete. Paul instructed Titus to "appoint elders in every city," then set forth the qualifications necessary for spiritual service in the church (Titus 1:5–9). Missing is any reference to appointing those who are, in modern jargon, "called to preach." I do not by any means deny the call to preach—I believe in it very strongly.[11] But while preaching is a vital and necessary gift for the church, it is never set forth as a requirement for serving as an elder within the church. An elder must be "able to teach" and able to "exhort in sound doctrine and to refute those who contradict"; there is no requirement that he be endowed with preaching gifts.[12] Some elders may be gifted in preaching, but all need not be. Elders must know the doctrines of Holy Scripture and be able to wield "the sword of the Spirit" in dialogue with others or in teaching settings; but the requirement of pulpit ministry is not laid upon them.

Here is precisely the wisdom of the New Testament pattern of plural eldership. No one man possesses all the gifts necessary for leading a congregation. Some men are endowed with strong pulpit gifts, but lack pastoral skills. Others excel in pastoral work of visiting and counseling, but are not strong when it comes to pulpit exposition. Some have unusual abilities in organizing and administrating the ministries of the church, but fail in pulpit and counseling skills. Some, to be sure, are multigifted and capable of enormous work at different levels. But the strain of tending to the entire ministry needs of the church can quickly deplete even the most gifted man.

The dilemma is that every church needs all of these skills—pulpit, pastoral, and administration—to serve the congregation's needs. Many churches don't have, of course, the resources to hire trained ministers to fill each gap. Far too often churches delay addressing ministry needs because they lack the finances to hire additional staff. Such delay becomes unnecessary if the New Testament pattern is followed. Indeed, every area of church need will be strengthened if a church patiently labors to bring together godly, gifted men who will serve with equality for the sake of the church's spiritual health and mission. Some of these men will be compensated as full-time or part-time ministers in the church, while others will serve *gratis* as part of their ministry as elders to the body of Christ.

Leadership by a plurality of godly men, accountable to one another, reduces the temptation for one man to wield excessive authority in the church or to use the church to satisfy his ego. Each man's weaknesses are complemented by the strengths of his fellow elders. Think of Paul's warning to the Ephesian elders (Acts 20:17–38). Not one man, but a group of elders were put on notice of the dangers awaiting their church. One man might cave in to the pressure of persecution. One man might fall prey to false teachers. One man might be overwhelmed by a variety of problems. In contrast, plural leadership increases the church's ability to stand firmly regardless of impediments to the faith. Mark Dever, Senior Pastor of Capitol Hill Baptist Church in Washington, D.C., and an elder in that congregation, advocates setting apart elders from within the local church. His comments on plurality offer a clear testimony to the effectiveness of this biblical pattern:

> Probably the single most helpful thing to my pastoral ministry among my church has been the recognition of the other elders [most of whom do not receive a salary from the church]. The service of the other elders along with me has had immense benefits. A plurality of elders should aid a church by rounding out the pastor's gifts, making up for some of his defects, supplementing his judgment, and creating support in the congregation for decisions, leaving leaders less exposed to unjust criticism. Such plurality also makes leadership more rooted and permanent, and allows for more mature continuity. It encourages the church to take more responsibility for the spiritual growth of its own members and helps make the church less dependent on its employees. Our own church in Washington has enjoyed these benefits and more because of God's gift to us of elders.[13]

THE SENIOR PASTOR AND ELDER PLURALITY

It is not suggested that the pastor be replaced, with elders divvying up the load. It is often, in fact, preferable that some within each church apply full-time energies to the labors of ministry, especially those that will be involved in the weekly ministry of proclamation. That seems to be the clear intimation of 1 Timothy 5:17: "The elders who rule well are to be considered worthy of double honor, *especially those who work hard at preaching and teaching*" (italics added). The "double honor" refers to "remuneration."[14] I spend an average of twenty-five to thirty hours weekly in preaching and teaching preparation. It is difficult, if not impossible, to maintain that kind of rigorous study schedule while employed in secular occupations and giving adequate attention to family needs. Elders do not replace the need for a senior pastor who labors in the Word and gives leadership to the church. Instead, elders come alongside the senior pastor as fellow servants to the body, filling the gaps in the pastor's weaknesses, holding up his arms as he preaches, sharing the burden for the multiplied pastoral needs in the church.

My fellow elders serve to protect me so that I can fulfill my calling and ministry. My summer schedule in 2002 was unusually packed. I led a mission trip; spent a week out of town, writing for an on-line journal; spoke for a week to six hundred kids at a youth camp; participated in a conference; directed our summer internship program; participated in a family vacation; and fulfilled normal ministry demands. A friend had asked me to lead a missions conference in his church during the fall, so I submitted this request to the elders. These men comprise the most supportive group with whom I've ever been associated. They encourage me to participate in ministry beyond our church. But in this case, they knew that I was beyond overload, so they told me that accepting this preaching assignment would not be a good decision. As much as I wanted to do the conference, especially on a topic much beloved, I accepted their decision as the wisest choice. As one of the elders told me, "Pastor, we want to protect you *from you*." And he was right on target. In God's providence, the very dates that I was to lead the missions conference were needed to travel out of town to minister to my father-in-law, who died shortly afterward. Those days will always be etched into my mind as precious time in helping a dying man. The Lord used my fellow elders to keep me on track so that I could best fulfill my ministry and, more importantly, maintain priority in ministering to my own family.

ELDER DUTIES

In some of my discussions with pastors and church leaders regarding elders, the question comes up, "Don't elders simply do the job of deacons in Baptist churches?" True, some churches have raised the bar of qualifications for their deacons so that they function as elders even though their title does not reflect it. It seems that most deacons, however, have been relegated to "board status"—dealing with problems with the water heater, deciding on re-striping the parking lot, approving the church youth trip, and so forth. These tasks are neither ignoble nor unnecessary. They are, in fact, quite important. But when the leadership group of a church is swamped in the mundane and temporal, they may fail to take to heart the deeper spiritual needs of the church. In the servant role, deacons take care of those mundane and temporal matters of church life so that elders are freed to concentrate upon spiritual matters. Deacons provide much needed wisdom and energy to the ample physical needs in the church, often using such provision as opportunities to minister as well to the spiritual needs of others.

But elders have a different focus. John Piper sums up the functions of elders under two headings: teaching and governing. "[Elders] are the doctrinal guardians of the flock and the overseers of the life of the church responsible to God for the feeding and care and ministry of the people."[15] Wayne Grudem concurs: "Elders, then, had responsibility to rule and to teach in New Testament churches."[16] While the inclusiveness of these categories seems appropriate, the duties of elders might better be approached in a fourfold manner: doctrine, discipline, direction, and distinction in modeling the Christian life.

- Doctrine
- Discipline
- Direction
- Distinction

The qualification distinguishing elders from deacons is the elders' aptness to teach, and ability to engage others doctrinally, even those in disagreement (1 Tim. 3:2; Titus 1:9). Attention to *doctrine* assures the church that their spiritual leaders are guarding the flock against "savage wolves" that would attack them to subvert their faith (Acts 20:28–30). But elders are not just guards; they are teachers of truth as well. Shepherding the flock of God requires feeding the church upon the rich truths of God's Word (1 Peter 5:2).

The elders at my church regularly discuss the contents of pulpit and classroom teaching. They help me in planning my preaching schedule so that I address "the whole purpose of God" in my pulpit ministry (Acts 20:27). We also work together in planning the ongoing training that our church offers in the broad range of Christian disciplines and ministries, as well as putting together conferences and seminars to profit the church and community. At the encouragement of our elders, I am presently engaged in preaching through the gospel of Matthew on Sunday mornings, and through Judges on Sunday evenings. Our Sunday school has just completed a study in Acts and will now embark on studying selected Psalms with a study of Ephesians to follow—again at the direction of the elders. Our Wednesday night schedule includes historical and theological studies; topics related to family, evangelism, apologetics, and personal issues; preparation for mission trips; classes on how to study the Bible; and studies on the spiritual disciplines, all recommended and usually taught by our elders. With a desire that our church grasps every genre of biblical literature and becomes equipped in the broad facets of spiritual disciplines, the elders help to map out a plan of *doctrine* for the church.

Coupled with doctrine is the matter of *discipline.* The word conveys the idea of training, admonishing, encouraging, correcting, and, at times, removing someone from church membership. Church discipline has grown out of favor in most circles but it is critical for maintaining healthy congregations.[17] While this is the work of the entire church (Matt. 18:15–20; Gal. 6:1–2), the elders must shoulder the burden to ensure the health of the church. Again, this falls under the role of shepherding as well as keeping watch over the souls of the congregation (Heb. 13:17). If a pastor stands alone in bringing a matter of church discipline to the church, opponents will likely skewer him! But the strength of godly leaders within the church, standing together in dealing with such matters, urges the entire church to recognize the seriousness of discipline. In those few times that we have taken church discipline to its ultimate point, our elders have prayed and wept together over the spiritual condition of those under discipline long before presenting them to the church for action of dismissal.

A fellow pastor bemoaned the divisiveness of a couple who attended his church and who constantly agitated destructive issues in the church. He told me that he was not sure how he needed to handle the situation, but he understood that action needed to be taken soon or he would have larger problems on his hands. This pastor is fortunate in that he has elders in his church. I suggested that he direct the elders to call this couple in for counsel and warning, so that the elders as a group might bear this burden and not the pastor alone. The elders could decide a course of action to protect the church from division and also protect their pastor from becoming embroiled in controversy.

Direction involves decision making, planning, administrating, delegating, and even governing the details of church life. This is where the work of shepherding includes not only feeding but also giving direction to the flock (1 Peter 5:2). Perhaps this work of shepherding and feeding is why the term *overseer* is used interchangeably with *elder*, since the ancient overseers were involved in directing those under their charge. Paul speaks of this task of direction when exhorting the Thessalonian believers to esteem those laboring as spiritual leaders among them who "have charge over you in the Lord and give you instruction" (1 Thess. 5:12–13). To "have charge over" refers specifically to leading and directing the church.[18] Additionally, the assertion that elders "rule" the church indicates they will "be at the head (of), rule, direct, . . . manage."[19] Some have abused this "rule" concept by prying into every facet of their members' lives. But spiritual leaders have no cause to manipulate or control the flock that belongs to a greater Shepherd.[20] Lording one's position and authority in the church is strictly forbidden (1 Peter 5:3). The writer of Hebrews calls these spiritual leaders "the ones leading you," giving the distinct impression of regular direction in ministry (Heb. 13:17). Directing the flock is no stale and stiff business, but calls for regular involvement and intimate knowledge of the church. That's why James instructs the scattered saints to "call for the elders of the church" in order to pray for sick members (James 5:14). Elders must seek to know the needs of the flock, understanding its strengths and weaknesses, while recognizing its spiritual gifts and ministry inclinations. The most daunting of responsibilities for elders involves the *distinction* of modeling the Christian life. Elders are to be examples to the flock, which is the reason for immediate public censure when one falls into public sin (1 Tim. 5:19–21). Peter told the elders "to be examples to the flock" (1 Peter 5:3). The writer of Hebrews reminds those struggling believers to reflect upon those who had been leading them (perhaps they were deceased or even martyred) and "imitate their faith" (Heb. 13:7). This plea to imitate is another reason for the detailed description of the character qualities of elders. It is not that any of the qualities, with the exception of aptitude for teaching, are beyond the norm for all Christians. Instead, elders are to set the example by modeling the blamelessness that ought to characterize all who know Christ (1 Tim. 3:2; Titus 1:6).

What difference can elders make in church life? If a congregation has a group of godly spiritual leaders who walk with Christ, who do so in such a way that they assist the body in fleshing out the details of the Christian life, who attend to the doctrine of the church, who labor to maintain discipline of the members, and who regularly give direction to the church, that church will be better positioned for spiritual growth and effective ministry.

REFLECTIONS

- What is the challenge for modern church government in light of God's Word?
- What are three titles used for plural eldership, and how does each shade the meaning of the office?
- How is the plurality of elders taught in the New Testament?
- What are the strengths of plurality in the local church?
- What are the fourfold duties of elders?

CHAPTER THREE

Character and Congregationalism

Why do we need spiritual leaders known as elders and deacons in our churches? With the high education level, the vast experience, and the varied abilities possessed by the average church member, why do we even need to have men in positions of elder and deacon? And considering the size of most congregations—less than 100 members—why bother with elders and deacons? Would it not be easier for one man to take care of the church?

One man serving as pastor cannot take care of all the needs in any ministry. Some churches expect as much—since that is the reason they employ him. But the living organism known as the local church has far too many needs and opportunities of service and growth for one man to capably meet. He might excel at preaching, but fall short on ministering to those in crisis. He might maintain regular hours for counseling while neglecting to plan, direct, and equip the church. Often the pastor becomes the brunt of criticism because he fails to wear enough hats to satisfy the needs (and sometimes whims) of the congregation. The church can have unrealistic expectations upon the solitary pastor, and the pastor can agonize with feelings of inadequacy for not fulfilling the church's expectations. But there is a better way.

Every situation a church faces calls for the Word of God. From time to time an issue may arise that the Word does not address directly, although typically answers can be found by inference. But for other areas, Scripture clearly gives an answer. Certainly, the issue of elders and deacons is such a case.

SURVEYING ACTS

The official designation of elders and deacons did not begin immediately in the early church. There was no formation committee or announcement that precipitated elders and deacons. Instead, we see the emergence of what some have termed "deacon prototypes" in "The Seven" of Acts 6, and even a prototype of the ministry of elders in "The Twelve," as they labored in the Word and prayer. The former group focused upon the temporal needs of the church (feeding the widows), while the latter sought to teach and govern the church. The early chapters of Acts refer to the apostles without reference to elders. Then in chapter 11 there is a reference to "the elders" (v. 30). Not until Acts 14:23 are "elders" intentionally appointed for the first time in the infant church: "And when they had appointed elders for them in every church, having prayed with fasting, they commended them to the Lord in whom they had believed." These young, small churches of Asia Minor needed biblical instruction, regular discipline, spiritual leadership, and models for the faith. So the apostle Paul saw the need for assuring the continued spiritual growth of these churches, appointing elders (plural) in every church (singular). This in itself offers an excellent pattern.

In Acts 15:2, the apostles are joined by elders as the spiritual leaders in Jerusalem. From this point onward in the book of Acts, elders became the norm. While there is no mention of deacons in the book of Acts, they are considered as part of the official leadership of the church at Philippi (Phil. 1:1) as Paul addresses that young church. Deacons were clearly to be an important part of the spiritual service in Ephesus under Timothy's pastoral charge (1 Tim. 3). In the epistles of Paul, Peter, James, John, the book of Hebrews, and the Revelation, significant passages refer to spiritual leaders of congregations. No one portion of Scripture relates everything concerning these spiritual leaders, but taken together these passages form a marvelous working structure of true, New Testament church life.

WHY ELDERS AND DEACONS?

Why Do We Need Elders and Deacons?

- It's the New Testament church's pattern.
- It assures congregations of well-rounded, balanced ministry.
- It meets diverse congregational needs through functioning in plurality.
- It strengthens the church's unity and efficiency.

While deacons are not the subject of this present work, it is not without use to reflect for a moment upon both offices of the church—elders and deacons.

1. *Elders and deacons are needed because that is the pattern taught in the early church.* The early churches serve as role models for the structure and leadership of present-day churches. Rather than simply structuring today's churches in a clever but nonbiblical fashion, churches need to adhere to the practice of Scripture. For evangelicals who believe in the sufficiency of Scripture for life and practice, it only makes sense to develop church polity based on God's Word.

2. *Elders and deacons are needed to assure congregations that the "whole person" will receive effective ministry.* Responsibilities of elders and deacons certainly overlap at times—deacons will indeed find plenty of spiritually oriented work while elders will at times deal with temporal issues—yet those two offices are distinct in their essential duties.

3. *Scripture does not specify a precise number of elders and deacons to be appointed in the church, only stating the office in the plural (two or more) rather than the singular.* If diverse congregations, like the more mature and larger Jerusalem church, and the weaker, smaller Lystra church both needed elders, then it is apparent that churches of every size and geographical locale do, too. The passage of time does not diminish the spiritual or temporal needs of those making

up the church. The New Testament does not distinguish church types or sizes or required maturity before needing elders and deacons.

4. *Establishing groups of elders and deacons gives the church an opportunity to function under God-given authority, keeping the church headed in the proper direction, building the unity of the body, and increasing efficiency in ministry.*

There appears to be no single way that elders were chosen in the early church. As one writer points out, "Much of the instruction given about church order is *ad hoc* rather than of universal principle."[1] So it must be understood what is principled and what is flexible. It is clear that Paul and Barnabas chose the first elders among the young churches in Asia Minor (Acts 14:23, where *appointed* means either "to elect by show of hands" or "to appoint"[2]). Whether the congregation affirmed their decision or not can only be speculated but it seems that affirmation *might* have occurred. In the earlier case of the deacon prototypes of Acts 6, the language implies congregational involvement in the decision-making process. They were told to "select from among you seven men" (v. 3), with selection carrying the idea of inspecting or examining the men for selection to this office.[3] The congregation no doubt was involved in the process, evidently putting forth the names of seven men who met with the apostolic approval. The precise way they did this is not given.

ELDERS AND CHARACTER

In the Pastoral Epistles, the office of overseer is something that a man might "aspire" to embrace (1 Tim. 3:1). But does he just volunteer to serve as elder? The list of character qualities no doubt means that the church is involved in some kind of examination of those aspiring to serve as elders, or otherwise spiritual wolves would gain ready entrance into church leadership. Elders who deserve public censure for failing to uphold the character and practice incumbent on those holding this office are rebuked before the entire church. They can be accused publicly but only by two or three witnesses lest there be unfounded charges leveled against them (1 Tim. 5:19–21). Such examination and censure at least suggests that elders ultimately serve at the pleasure of the congregation. In the process of forming the church in Crete, Titus was told to "appoint elders in every city" (Titus 1:5). The word *appoint* seems to have taken on ecclesiastical strength as it implies something akin to ordaining the elders to office. Did Titus single out the men without the congregation's involvement? Or does the appointment suggest that Titus availed himself of the churches' voices in the process but final discretion for appointment was left to him? The ambiguity of the language and settings prevent a definitive response.

When it comes to the selection of elders (or deacons) in the church, it is perhaps best to leave the process to the individual, autonomous churches. Flexibility seems to be in order, but an elimination process would assure elder candidates to be qualified for office. Eliminating candidates will be difficult to accomplish at a congregational level because of the intensive and personal nature of examination required. But at the minimum, congregations should be involved in nominating men deemed faithful and qualified to be elders. Nominees would then undergo examination by a smaller group (the presbytery or ordination council) responsible for recommendation to the office of elder.

The bar must be raised for elders and deacons if these officers are to serve their respective churches as they ought.

What qualifies a man for the office of elder in a local church? In my observation, the greatest oversight by churches considering elders—or even churches that have deacons functioning as elders—is neglect of biblical qualifications. In regard to requirements for elders and deacons, the bar must be raised if these officers are to serve their respective churches as they ought. Nothing is, in fact, more important than examining men in light of the qualifications set forth in 1 Timothy 3 and Titus 1, and expecting those men to maintain faithfulness in these qualities. In church settings where shifting to elder leadership might create undue conflict, it is recommended to raise the bar for, at the very least, spiritual qualifications for leaders. Churches that simply fill a vacant leadership slot without seriously considering the nominees' qualifications set the stage for deeper problems. As John Piper expressed, "Spiritual qualifications should never be sacrificed to technical expertise."[4] Gerald Cowen adds, "For the church to have a moral impact on society, the highest standards should be upheld."[5] Adding public speakers, accountants, legal experts, project managers, banking executives, and advertising geniuses is not the object of spiritual leadership. Some of those qualified might have additional technical expertise of this kind, but such must always be secondary.

---

1 Timothy 3:1–7

It is a trustworthy statement: if any man aspires to the office of overseer, it is a fine work he desires to do. An overseer, then, must be above reproach, the husband of one wife, temperate, prudent, respectable, hospitable, able to teach, not addicted to wine or pugnacious, but gentle, peaceable, free from the love of money. He must be one who manages his own household well, keeping his children under control with all dignity (but if a man does not know how to manage his own household, how will he take care of the church of God?), and not a new convert, so that he will not become conceited and fall into the condemnation incurred by the devil. And he must have a good reputation with those outside the church, so that he will not fall into reproach and the snare of the devil.

The chief characteristic of an elder is being "above reproach." Paul demands this: "An overseer, then, *must* be above reproach" [emphasis added].[6] The phrase *above reproach* serves as an umbrella under which the balance rests. "It *doesn't* mean that a man has to be perfect," writes John MacArthur. "If so, we would all be disqualified! It means that there must not be any great blot on his life that others might point to."[7] Piper adds, "The word seems to be a general word for living in a way that gives no cause for others to think badly of the church or of the faith or the Lord. . . . The focus here is not a person's relationship to the Lord, but how others see him."[8] A man known as a hothead or a womanizer or a shady business-dealer or loose with his tongue has no place among the eldership.

The phrase *husband of one wife* has over the years generated much print. Many commentators give detailed arguments of its meaning so there is no need here to work through all the issues regarding this quality. But in order not to get lost in the arguments, the phrase literally means "a one-woman-man," pointing to the fidelity in the marriage relationship as well as the ongoing devotion exemplified toward his wife. In a day of rampant moral failure within church leadership, it is critical that elders set the example for faithfulness and devotion in their marriages. Is there a reason to question the elder candidate's devotion to his wife? If so, then he should not be placed in a position of leadership.

The word *temperate* refers to the ability of an elder to exercise self-control over his appetites so that they do not dictate his life, whether regarding alcohol (as the original meaning) or the broader desires of the flesh. The elder is thus to be sober-minded in all things. *Prudent* implies that an elder's mind remains engaged, that he is able to exercise sound judgment even in difficult times. *Respectable* implies that the elder's personal life is well ordered, reflected in relationships with others. He does not engage in pretenses, but conscientiously guards his inner life so that his outward conduct might bring honor to Christ and the gospel. An elder is also to be *hospitable,* a word that originally meant a lover of strangers. His home must be opened to others as a center of ministry beyond the walls of the church building.

The elder's aptitude to teach (1 Tim. 3:2; Titus 1:9) is central to his work. Some divide elders into categories of ruling elders and teaching elders, based on 1 Timothy 5:17: "The elders who rule well are to be considered worthy of double honor, especially those who work hard at preaching and teaching." Without question, elders are involved in the ruling aspect of church life—that goes with the office. But all are to be involved in the teaching ministry of the church. It can be argued that some excel in teaching while others excel in governing, but to make a distinction seems artificial. The necessary balance of both teaching and governing keeps the entire group of elders focused on the Scriptures, thus deriving wisdom from the Word, and applying the lessons and principles of Scripture in congregational life. Doing so calls for all elders to be theologically astute, biblically articulate, and ready to instruct individuals or groups as the need arises. An elder who only knows how to "rule," and lacks the biblical precision called for in the aptitude of teaching, will likely create disharmony among the elders. Nothing has honed our elders more than all of us being students of Scripture and accountable for teaching the church.

"Freedom from enslavements should be so highly prized that no bondage is yielded to," explains John Piper concerning the implications of "not addicted to wine."[9] So while this characteristic stresses that an elder must not "sit long at his wine" or be "a slave to drink," he also must guard other areas where he might be tempted to enslavement.[10] Self-control will also be shown in the elder's temper. Therefore, he is not to be "pugnacious," or a bully, but instead "gentle," or kind and forbearing, and "peaceable," going to great lengths to avoid unnecessary conflict in the church. "Free from the love of money" reminds elders of the temporal nature of material things, and the enslaving tendencies found when possessions become the focus of life. Generosity, contentment, and personal financial discipline serve to cure love of money.

"He must be one who manages his own household well, keeping his children under control with all dignity (but if a man does not know how to manage his own household, how will he take care of the church of God?)." The elder must set the example of spiritual leadership in the home. John Piper explains:

> The home is a proving ground for ministry. [The elder] should have submissive children. This does not mean perfect, but it does mean well disciplined, so that they do not blatantly and regularly disregard the instructions of their parents. The children should revere the father (*meta pases semnotetos*) [sic]. He should be a loving and responsible spiritual leader in the home. His wife should be respected and tenderly loved. Their relationship should be openly admirable.[11]

Since spiritual maturity is at the heart of an elder's life, Paul warns that he must not be a new convert, "so that he will not become conceited and fall into the condemnation incurred by the devil." Nothing seems to puff up an immature person more than a title. The eyes of the church are constantly on the elders, seeking exemplary conduct and instruction. Putting a new believer into such a demanding role positions him to slip into the Devil's trap of pride.

An elder represents his church, so "he must have a good reputation with those outside *the church,* so that he will not fall into reproach and the snare of the devil" (emphasis added). The world is not setting standards for the church's leaders but, to be sure, the church's leaders must never slip below even the world's standards of character, dignity, and propriety. The high standards of Christian life and character must give the world no cause for accusation of hypocrisy in the church's leaders.

Paul's list of character qualities penned to Titus resembles that penned to Timothy but with some variations. Thus, the apostle was giving a sample in each epistle of what Christian character looks like when taken seriously. Again, "above reproach" stands as a sentinel over the balance of the character requirements. While the language in Titus regarding the family differs slightly from that in Timothy, the intention remains the same. The elder is to set an example by wisely ordering his own home: "the husband of one wife, having children who believe, not accused of dissipation or rebellion."

Titus 1:5–9

For this reason I left you in Crete, that you would set in order what remains and appoint elders in every city as I directed you, namely, if any man is above reproach, the husband of one wife, having children who believe, not accused of dissipation or rebellion. For the overseer must be above reproach as God's steward, not self-willed, not quick-tempered, not addicted to wine, not pugnacious, not fond of sordid gain, but hospitable, loving what is good, sensible, just, devout, self-controlled, holding fast the faithful word which is in accordance with the teaching, so that he will be able both to exhort in sound doctrine and to refute those who contradict.

Again, John Piper provides helpful commentary that explains Paul's meaning regarding the children of elders:

> Here, the focus is not just on the relationship of the children to the father, but on their behavior in general. They are not to be guilty of the accusation of "wild living" or uncontrolled behavior. And they are not to be "insubordinate."
>
> Does *pista* mean "believing" (with RSV) or "faithful" in the sense of honest and trustworthy? In favor of the latter would be the use of the word in 1 Timothy 3:11, where women (deaconesses or wives of deacons) are to be *pistas en pasin*, faithful in all things. Other places in the pastoral epistles [sic] where the word seems to have this meaning are 1 Timothy 1:12, 15; 3:1; 4:9; 2 Timothy 2:11; 2:13; Titus 1:9; 3:8.
>
> So the idea seems to be of children who are well bred, orderly, generally obedient, responsible, and reliable.[12]

Paul continues, repeating the need for an elder's being "above reproach," but in this case the reason is because he is "God's steward." The term points to the ongoing responsibility of the elder to manage the affairs of the church. If encumbered by areas of reproach or constantly trying to hide his behavior, then he will not fare well as a manager of a spiritual body. In Titus, Paul adds that an elder is not to be "self-willed," that is, never to be so stubborn about his own opinions that he is unteachable and unbending or thinking only of himself.[13] Nor is he to be "quick-tempered," or in the habit of firing his attitude and tongue quickly when someone contradicts him. Instead, he is to be marked by "loving what is good, sensible, just, devout, self-controlled." His priorities are fixed on the things that matter: relationships, justice, purity, and intense devotion to the Lord. The list is crowned by "self-control," a term meaning "complete self-mastery, which controls all passionate impulses and keeps the will loyal to the will of God."[14]

While Paul tells Timothy that elders must be "able to teach," he amplifies the meaning in his letter to Titus: "Holding fast the faithful word which is in accordance with the teaching"; that is, he not only understands biblical doctrine but is diligent in applying the same to his life and practice. Elders must be students of Scripture, faithful in reading and studying bible doctrine, regular in delving deeper into the Word, thereby setting the example of loving God's Word for the congregation. Elders' faithfulness in the Word enables them to "be able both to exhort in sound doctrine"—teach, admonish, and instruct whether one-on-one or to groups—"and to refute those who contradict"—that is, they readily deal with error and false teaching as well as correcting those who misapply God's Word for some selfish or legalistic motive.

The most remarkable thing about these characteristics is that there is nothing remarkable about them.

—D. A. Carson

In order to avoid self-scrutiny, some have magnified the seeming impossibility of these character qualities, stressing that no one fulfills them. But in both the 1 Timothy and Titus texts Paul is calling upon elders to simply act like genuine Christians. Outside the need for teaching, none of the characteristics should be unusual among Christians—every believer should seek to be "above reproach." In a sermon, D. A. Carson said, as I recall, "The most remarkable thing about these characteristics is that there is nothing remarkable about them." They demonstrate that the elder takes seriously the gospel's intent of sanctifying a people for God's own possession (Titus 2:14).

Elders not only lead the congregation, but they also must work with each other. The character qualities thus remain critical for plural leadership to live in unity and work together in humility. Alexander Strauch clearly expressed this need:

When it functions properly, shared leadership requires a greater exercise of humble servanthood than does unitary leadership. In order for an eldership to operate effectively, the elders must show mutual regard for one another, submit themselves one to another, patiently wait upon one another, genuinely consider one another's interests and perspectives, and defer to one another. Eldership, then, enhances brotherly love, humility, mutuality,

patience, and loving interdependence—qualities that are to mark
the servant church.[15]

> The goal of a church should not be to establish plural
> eldership at any cost, but rather to elevate the standards of
> spiritual leadership in the church at any cost.

It would be wise for any church pursuing a transition to elder leadership to spend time emphasizing the character more than even the function of elders. Functions will vary from church to church but the character
of a holy, humble servant life should always mark those set apart as elders. Elders, deacons, and other church officers that fail to display the
character required of spiritual leaders have done great damage to
churches. Therefore, set forth God's standards—raise the bar of qualifications to a level that parallels the teaching of Scripture. Even congregations that are not sure what constitutes the function of elders will more
likely follow elder leadership when it resides in men who truly live like
Christians. The goal of a church should not be to establish plural eldership at any cost, but rather to elevate the standards of spiritual leadership in the church at any cost.

PLURALITY IN CONGREGATIONAL FRAMEWORK

In the process of elevating spiritual leadership, churches must pursue
biblical patterns for our churches, including plural eldership. But some
fear the term *elders*. One Southern Baptist leader stated his stark opposition: "I am not in favor of elder rule in the Southern Baptist church to
which I belong, indeed, if the church to which I belong instituted elder
rule, I would leave."[16] During the past dozen years a number of Baptist
churches have adopted plural eldership in one form or another—although
not all did so smoothly. Some churches have split over the issue because
of the strong feelings and fears of jettisoning the cherished Baptist practice of congregationalism. Pastors have even been dismissed or barred
from the fellowship of their local associations over eldership.

Growing up in a Southern Baptist church, I found that elders were foreign to our polity. The local Church of Christ congregations had elders that so firmly ruled their churches, the ministers served at their pleasure. That picture of "totalitarian rule" by elders put fear in a Baptist's mind! In other churches the elders lacked the spiritual dignity of the office, thus negatively coloring the office of elder. Still others appeared to have weak elders who lacked the passion that ought to characterize spiritual leadership. Here, then, is precisely where the problem of fear arises— getting our picture of elders from sources other than the Bible. By adopting plural elder leadership, many Baptists thus fear the loss of congregationalism, while many pastors fear the loss of authority.

These fears are understandable. But as in any situation that causes fear, stepping back, taking an unbiased look, and evaluating it by the facts can often alleviate anxiety. I might fear a snake in the path ahead of me. But if I stop to realize that, first, it is probably not poisonous; second, the snake fears me more than I fear it; and third, I can go around the snake, then I need not tremble and profusely sweat. Facts change my entire outlook.

Plural eldership should not eliminate congregationalism. It is true that some forms of plural eldership completely by-pass the congregation. In the early church, however, the congregation was involved to some degree in all decisions. The church is to hold the final authority, for instance, on matters of disciplining its membership (Matt. 18:15–17; 1 Cor. 5). The church selected the deacon-prototypes upon the counsel of the apostles, thus providing a workable pattern for congregational involvement in recommending spiritual and temporal leaders (Acts 6:1–5). After the apostles and elders established the church's position regarding the problem raised by the Judaizers, the congregation became involved by approving the recommendation of sending messengers to the churches of Asia Minor as the official voice of the Jerusalem church. The congregation as a whole was not part of the discussions or debates, but they were later informed, and affirmed the result of the council: "Then it seemed good to the apostles and the elders, with the whole church, to choose men from among them to send to Antioch with Paul and Barnabas" (Acts 15:22). *Then it seemed good* was a political term in the Greek world for "voting" or "passing a measure in the assembly."[17]

There is no evidence that the early church voted on every issue. Rather, the plural eldership competently and efficiently handled day-to-day matters. And the church respected and submitted to this leadership, knowing that trustworthy men stood before them by divine design. On occasion, the churches had to be reminded to obey and submit to the plural eldership, but that eldership, then, lacked despotic purposes in the early church, and the congregation exercised decisive roles in church life (1 Thess. 5:12–13; Heb. 13:17). Congregationalism certainly existed, but not to such a degree that the public assembly literally ran the church.

Absolute congregational government is unwieldy in practice. During my early years of ministry, a seminary president told a group of young, aspiring ministers that if a church *voted* to call you as pastor then you had best go, because that was the will of God. I was shocked by his tone—and I still am—and by his insistence that the will of God is infallibly known through the congregation's vote. A little reading of church history refutes such an idea. Church votes are affected by human depravity as much as are individuals. Church votes cannot assure God's mind. Mark Dever offers a reminder that congregations must labor to understand the teaching of Scripture rather than presuming blanket infallibility when the church assembles:

> A church is not just straightforward democracy, for in churches there is a common recognition of our fallen state, of our tendency to err, and, on the other hand, of the *in*errancy of God's Word. So the members of a church congregation are democratic, perhaps, only in the sense that they work as a congregation to try to understand God's Word.[18]

The eldership will lead the charge in understanding God's Word. As students of Scripture and men devoted to prayer, elders earn the congregation's trust and enhance their authority as spiritual leaders in the church. The authority of leaders is necessary in a church, as it is in any type of government. While national, state, and local governments serve at the pleasure of their citizens, the citizens depend on their elected officials to give leadership, direction, and protection on a daily basis. Citizens submit to this authority because it gives order to their lives. In the same way, the congregation that submits to elder leadership can function with greater order and purpose. The congregation holds the eldership accountable to exercise faithfully their responsibilities under the Lord Jesus Christ. "The ministry of the church," writes John Piper, "is primarily the work of the members in the activity of worship toward God, nurture toward each other and witness toward the world. Internal structures for church governance are *not* the main ministry of the church, but are the necessary equipping and mobilizing of the saints for the work of ministry."[19] So the congregation at large must focus on mobilization for ministry rather than spend its time worrying over governance. That responsibility is entrusted to the smaller body of the elders. Piper adds, "Governance structures should be lean and efficient to this end, not aiming to include as many people as possible in office-holding, but to free and fit as many people as possible for ministry."[20]

At the root of much opposition to plural eldership are pastors who fear the loss of their authority in the church. Although many Baptist churches claim to exercise congregationalism, their actual structure is monarchical episcopacy—the solitary rule of one man over the congregation. Early Baptists reacted against monarchical episcopacy in the Church of Rome and the Church of England. Their dissenting voice echoed with other seventeenth-century evangelicals who were alarmed over the abuse levied by the solitary rule of one man over the church. Baptists vested congregations with final authority in matters of church life, but also recognized the need for order that comes only through spiritual leadership. The Philadelphia Confession of Faith (1742) provides a good example of both congregational voice and the authority entrusted to its spiritual leaders:

[Article] 8. A particular church gathered, and completely organized, according to the mind of Christ, consists of officers and members: and the officers appointed by Christ to be chosen and set apart by the church (so called and gathered) for the peculiar administration of ordinances and execution of power or duty, which He entrusts them with or calls them to, to be continued to the end of the world, are bishops or elders, and deacons.

[Article] 9. The way appointed by Christ for the calling of any person, fitted and gifted by the Holy Spirit, unto office of bishop or elder in the Church is, that he be chosen thereunto by the

common suffrage of the Church itself; and solemnly set apart by
fasting and prayer, with the imposition of hands of the leadership of the Church, if there be any before constituted therein:
and of a deacon, that he be chosen by the like suffrage, and set
apart by prayer, and the imposition of hands.[21]

The officers of the church, elders and deacons, are appointed by Christ
and chosen by the church. They possess the "execution of power or duty,
which He entrusts them with or calls them to." Each elder is "chosen
thereunto by the common suffrage"—or voting—"of the Church itself."
So the pastor does not lack authority, but rather he shares authority with
the plurality of spiritual leaders chosen by the church.

Is this shared authority to be feared by a pastor who has been called to
serve vocationally in a church? Not if the elders adhere to the biblical requirements for character and practice. Instead, a pastor should welcome
this structure as a God-given means for protecting him and enhancing the
ministry of the church. Granted, major problems will arise when unqualified men serve as elders. But that is part of the ongoing struggle faced by
the church until Christ returns. The pastor must labor to preach, teach,
train, and pray until the Lord purifies the church's leadership base, making
it possible for the pastor gladly to share authority with a plural eldership.

Another element of the fear-factor involves the concept of "ruling." If
ruling means dictatorial control over church members' lives—including
constant prying into mundane personal decisions, or placing demands
on members outside the parameters of church ministry—then that type
of rule is well to be feared. Indeed, rule of that sort has given bad press to
plural eldership and is a distortion of the biblical picture of elders. Elders are never to rule in a "lording" manner; rather they are to serve the
church in humility. Elder rule must never resemble the despotic rule of
Henry VIII or any number of Stalinist dictators. Instead, it must mirror
the shepherd-rule modeled by Christ. Shepherding the flock of God does
demand the exercise of a level of governance, but elders must exercise
that governance as those who will give account to the Chief Shepherd of
His flock (1 Peter 5:2–5; Heb. 13:17).

*Plural eldership serves to prevent one man from falling prey to the tempta-
tion of dominating a congregation.* Shared authority hones the focus and

spirituality of the elders. A pastor who is called by a church will certainly hold greater responsibility than the other elders because of the duties entrusted to him. In this case the pastor is first among equals in authority—first by virtue of the church's call and his training and gifts, but equal in that he is not a "Lone Ranger" figure in church leadership. Daniel Wallace explains that "accountability and our sin natures" provide one of the clearest reasons for the shared authority of plural eldership. He continues,

> Each leader knows that he lacks complete balance, that there are things he continues to struggle with. Further, even beyond the sin nature factor is the personality factor. Some pastors are detail men; others are big picture men. Some love music, others have gotten little from music. . . . All of us together contribute to the way the body of Christ works. But a church that follows in lock-step with the personality and foibles of one man will always be imbalanced.
>
>   . . . *Churches that have a pastor as an authority above others (thus, in function, a monarchical episcopate) have a disproportionately high number of moral failures at the top level of leadership.* In other words, it is less likely for a pastor to fall into sin if he is *primus inter parus* ("first among equals" in the sense of his visibility and training, not spirituality) than if he is elevated above the rest of the leadership.[22]

Plural Eldership
- Encourages leaders by shouldering the load of ministry
- Approaches ministry with greater precision
- Curtails tyranny and authoritarianism in the church
- Provides a laboratory for displaying unity in the church

Developing plural leadership is demanding, so some may ask, *Why bother?* A plurality offers each elder some measure of encouragement since the body of elders or body of deacons work together on behalf of their particular congregation. Each man is to work toward the same purpose.

They can lift up one who is under pressure or offer a word of consolation to one who has a need. Many times I've watched as our elders have helped each other shoulder difficult loads or labored with each other in prayer.

In my own experience I know what it is to stand alone in a congregation—virtually every pastor knows what I mean. It is a difficult and trying time when a pastor is seeking to follow the teaching of God's Word and there is no crowd rushing to join him. But how marvelous and uplifting it is to have like-minded and like-purposed brethren standing with you. It breathes encouragement into any Christian leader's heart.

A plurality provides the opportunity to approach the whole work of ministry in a more exacting way. In a body of elders or body of deacons, each man will inevitably have his own particular gifts and strengths to add to the overall work. When laboring as a team, each man can apply his gifts to the common good of the entire body. No one man attempts to carry the load of a congregation.

A plurality, too, curtails attempts at tyranny or dictatorships. Having too much authority and too little accountability corrupts some people. This is especially true in the spiritual realm. When someone lacks spiritual maturity, that person's role in leadership can provide opportunities for ego-boosting or power-grabbing. Plural leadership protects against such abuses because the leaders hold one another accountable for purity of motives and actions. Equal authority among the elders checks attempts by one man to dominate the church leadership.

Plurality also serves as a laboratory for proving unity. Any group of people working together for a period of time will have its unity tested. The elders' character, or lack thereof, will surface during times of testing and adversity. Nothing is any sweeter than to see brethren walk through such times in unity.

REFLECTIONS

- Why do we need both elders and deacons?
- How were elders selected in the early church? Does this offer an example of how elder selection should be conducted in our day?
- What qualifies a man to be an elder? Identify the chief characteristics.
- Why do some church leaders fear plural eldership?

PART TWO

Three Key Biblical Texts

CHAPTER FOUR

A Model for Our Times

Acts 20:17–31

Why appoint elders and deacons as spiritual leaders in the church? When Paul addressed Timothy on the subject of elders and deacons, he concluded his remarks with the assertion, "I write so that *you will know how one ought to conduct himself in the household of God,* which is the church of the living God, the pillar and support of the truth" (1 Tim. 3:15, emphasis added). The clear inference is that the way to "conduct" or discharge the duties of the church includes the ministry of elders and deacons. This passage sheds light on the whole question of spiritual leadership. Paul wanted to give Timothy clear instructions on the functioning of the church. In 1 Timothy 2, he dealt with the matter of prayer and worship, as well as questions that Timothy had probably asked about women. He dealt, too, with the ministry of teaching, reading of Scripture in the public worship, and warning the church of deceivers. He also addressed the church's responsibility toward widows, and he even gave a word on compensating spiritual leaders and how they must be dealt with in the case of open sin.

But central to the subject of discharging duties in the church is the functioning of elders and deacons. Although this text does not address the broad spectrum of elders' and deacons' work, it does address the qualifications for those offices. Evidently, their function was unquestioned at this point in the early church. Elders were already serving in Ephesus before Timothy assumed a leadership role in that church. Paul sought to ensure that the men serving in these two noble offices maintained a particular level of qualifications. It is interesting that his letter was delivered to help Timothy as he pastored the church at Ephesus.

Having been brought up in the Baptist church, I attended two churches during my adolescence, and both were quite traditional. These churches had senior pastors, deacons, and additional staff members, but elders were at other churches. To my knowledge, all who have Baptist backgrounds acknowledge the office of deacon without question. Although the London, Philadelphia, and New Hampshire Confessions, dating from the seventeenth through the nineteenth centuries, identify both offices of elders and deacons,[1] when it comes to the office of elder, Baptists tend to balk. When our church in Memphis was in the process of studying the biblical teaching on church leadership, including elders, one member stopped attending rather abruptly. I asked while visiting him at his home about his reason for leaving. He quickly pointed to the talk about elders. I asked him if he had a concern about elders. He replied simply, "It's just not Baptist!" Although I cited historical examples of elders in Baptist churches and pointed to the biblical teaching, he would not consider it even long enough to investigate the subject.

Yet the teaching of God's Word concerning elders guarding and leading the church, with the deacons coming alongside them to serve the church, demands thoughtful study. The biblical references to elders commonly are equated with the office of pastor or modern-day church staff. But that interpretation presents a hermeneutical problem: reading back into the ancient text our modern practices rather than understanding the Scripture in its historical context. Such is precisely what one opponent of elder leadership does when he claims that "all elder/overseers were ministry-oriented and laity-exclusive."[2] While it's true that the pastor is an elder, it is not necessarily fact that elders are only the "paid professionals." The church loses some of its greatest leadership assets when we neglect to place qualified men from the congregation at large as elders. It also smacks of arrogance to think that only the professionally trained can serve as spiritual leaders in the church. Proper functioning of elders only serves to strengthen the pastoral ministry of the church. John MacArthur explains that plural elder leadership—staff and non-staff—benefits the church: "Their combined counsel and wisdom helps assure that decisions are not self-willed or self-serving to a single individual (cf. Prov. 11:14)." He asserts, "In fact, one-man leadership is characteristic of cults, not the church."[3]

The apostle Paul understood this great need for godly leaders. On his second missionary journey, Paul came to the famous Asian city of Ephesus, "the chief city of the province," from which he would evangelize Asia Minor (Acts 19:10).[4] Ephesus was an important cultural and economic center in the Roman Empire, yet also an important center of pagan worship that featured the temple of Diana, "one of the Seven wonders of the ancient world."[5] There, Paul preached and a riot ensued! But God gave fruit for his labors so that a church was raised up in the city. The apostle stayed for three years, preaching and teaching the Word. During this period he evidently appointed elders to serve the church.

On his third missionary journey, Paul came near Ephesus, but because he had determined to go to Jerusalem, he did not land in Ephesus. Instead, he sailed past, landing at Miletus. From there, he called the Ephesian elders to meet him. In Acts 20:17–31, Luke records Paul's last encounter with these men, one that breathes with love and passion as the apostle gives final instructions for this church. Paul's message establishes an unmistakable need for elders to carry on the work of shepherding the church. It is important to see the heart of this text and recognize this same need in other churches. If elders played such a vital role in the cosmopolitan church in Ephesus, do we not have the same need today? Paul's exhortation to the Ephesian elders answers the question, "Why elders?"

Acts 20:17–31

- The Church's Common Need (Acts 20:17, 28–31)
- Shepherds for the Flock (Acts 20:28, 31)
- An Unforgettable Foundation (Acts 20:28)

THE CHURCH'S COMMON NEED (ACTS 20:17, 28–31)

Note the terms that Luke uses in recording Paul's exhortation. In verse 17, he calls this leadership body at Ephesus, "the elders of the church," that is, a plurality of elders serving one church. Some argue that the Ephesian church was divided into house churches, and the elders were simply the leaders of the house groups. But that does injustice to the text, as Paul called for "the elders of the church"—elders, plural; church, singular.[6] Then in verse 28, Paul states that the Holy Spirit "has made you overseers, to shepherd the church of God." *Overseers* is the same term that Paul uses in 1 Timothy 3:1, which the Authorized Version translates as "bishops" and the *New American Standard Bible* translates as "overseers." In Greek, the term is *episkopos*, while the designation "elder" is the Greek word *presbuteros*. He uses the word "shepherd" as a verb: to feed and care for the flock.[7] The Greek word used is *poimainō*, from which the noun "pastor," as used in Ephesians 4:11, has its roots. The point is that all three of these words are interchangeable. They do not refer to separate hierarchies or multitiered offices in the church, but to the same office or function within the local church. Peter likewise uses these term interchangeably in 1 Peter 5:1–2.[8]

As seen in chapter 2 of this current work, the distinction found in the term *elder* points to the character of the man, and was used of men advanced in maturity within the Jewish community. *Overseer* or *bishop* points to his function of spiritual leadership, as these terms were used in the Greek culture for commissioners or administrators of cities. The use of *pastor* typifies his ministry; the concept of shepherding a flock had abundant imagery throughout that part of the world.

Why was there a need for elders to serve in the church? The early church lived under external assault until about the fourth century. For three hundred years, opposition, attacks, and persecution fell upon the church, up to the reign of the Roman emperor Constantine. Those attacks came at various intervals in efforts to catch the church off-guard. Emperors Nero, Domitian, Trajan, and Hadrian oversaw legendary periods of persecution. But along with external persecution, corruption in doctrine, personalities, and leadership also brutalized the church[9]: "I know that after my departure savage wolves will come in among you, not sparing the flock" (Acts 20:29).

As long as Paul was among the Ephesian flock, he could easily recognize the attacks of the adversary and address them. He had the courage and authority to stand against whatever forces attacked the church. But Paul's presence among the Ephesian believers was coming to a close. Now they faced fresh opposition without the great apostle deflecting the blows. So Paul charges the Ephesian elders—and all who follow in their pattern—to take on this task of guarding the flock against assaults from without and within.

Paul uses strong terms to describe the attacks. He calls the perpetrators "savage wolves," depicting the Ephesian church as a flock of helpless sheep finding itself under the deadly attack of wolves (Acts 20:27). Christ used the same imagery in Matthew 7:15: "Beware of the false prophets, who come to you in sheep's clothing, but inwardly are ravenous wolves." Wolves, in this case, would have donned sheep's clothing so that by subterfuge they might subvert the church.

One recurring theme found in the epistles is the warning against false teachers. Some would claim to be "the Christ," others would have a new revelation, still others would teach a false gospel. And it is a sad fact that false teachers duped many. The Ephesian church was part of the seven churches of Asia Minor that our Lord addresses in Revelation 2–3. Most of those churches had fallen prey to spiritual lethargy, while some had given way to tolerating false teachers in their midst. Paul, through his epistles to Timothy (1 Tim. 4:1–3; 6:3–5; 2 Tim. 3), later warned the Ephesian church of false teachers.

When one considers that warnings about false teachers came from our Lord and from the pens of the New Testament writers Paul, John, Peter, and Jude, it ought to awaken us that false teaching remains a grave danger. Churches and individual Christians can fall prey to this attack, whether from outside or inside the body. If the church at Ephesus needed to have men guarding them from false teaching, I would say that the churches in Memphis or Dallas or Chicago or Baltimore need the same. In these particular warnings, personality conflicts were far from the apostle's mind. His concern centered on teaching that moved away from the veracity of Scripture to embrace a distorted faith. He charged the Ephesian elders to "be on guard for yourselves and for all the flock, among which the Holy Spirit has made you overseers, to shepherd the church of

God which He purchased with His own blood" (Acts 20:28). The shepherding process demands the ability to recognize wolves. What constitutes a "wolf-theology"?

- Teaching that in any way denies the deity of Christ or the coequality of the Trinity
- Teaching that substitutes anything for the sufficiency of the death of Christ in atoning for our sins
- Teaching that denies the need for God's justice being satisfied in order for sinners to be saved
- Teaching that robs God of glory by insisting that salvation is not totally a work of God's grace
- Teaching that denies the bodily resurrection of Christ
- Teaching that claims to have revelations that are not contained in the canons of the Old and New Testaments
- Teaching that insists upon some kind of work or self-denial or ascetic practice to improve one's standing before God rather than simply resting upon the merits of Christ

Is "wolf-theology" being taught today? Yes, indeed! I received a note from a pastor friend in Louisiana telling me about the president of a Baptist college in Georgia who authored a book denying the authority of Scripture, the virgin birth of Christ, the deity of Christ, the necessity of the Cross as the means of atoning for sin, and denying that human beings even have need of salvation. Even more distressing is that some Baptist churches allowed this man in their pulpit simply because he claims to be a Baptist. In such cases, the elders of the church have a responsibility to prevent even dignified looking wolves from deceiving the flock.

The weight of responsibility for recognizing false teaching, and then acting to correct or remove it, rests with the elders. The elders of the church have the task of constantly scrutinizing "every wind of doctrine" (Eph. 4:14). They are to be vigilant in recognizing false teaching, warning the body, and guarding the flock from falling prey (Heb. 13:17).

Paul was concerned not only with the attacks from outside the body, but also the deceit arising from within the body: "and from among your own selves men will arise, speaking perverse things, to draw away the disciples after them" (Acts 20:30). Just as there was a Judas among the twelve apostles, there are Judases in the church today. Such persons have self-centered motives for joining the church body. They seek to use the church for personal aggrandizement, to improve their sense of power or their material gain, and to draw disciples away from the truth.

Paul describes their pattern as "speaking perverse things," all with the goal of alienating (so expresses the Greek on this verb *draw away*) some of the believers from the rest of the church. The idea is aptly expressed by our common use of the term *perverse*, ideas that even children would recognize as immoral. But the word actually means, "to turn aside, to twist, to pervert, to distort."[10] "Perverse things" meant a perversion of the truth or a slight alteration of the truth. It involved taking that which was true, and then reshaping its meaning or giving it a false application, or manipulating it to say something other than its intended meaning. While the teaching of the "ravenous wolves" comes rather brazenly and is easily recognized, the teaching or "speaking" to which Paul refers in this passage is deceitful and difficult to recognize. It takes discernment in understanding human nature and understanding the Word of God to see the subtle shading of God's Word, thereby giving it alternative meanings—meanings that God did not intend. Once a Christian latches on to such distorted ideas of biblical truth, that person is easy prey for alienation from the rest of the church. He or she might view others in the church as unenlightened, and then follow the deceitful teaching to his or her own shame.

As evangelicals, we face no greater danger than deceit within the church. Evangelicals have been duped by nice smiles, charming words, and a little razzle-dazzle coming from deceivers. The great need of the hour is for godly men within our churches to be so sensitive to God's Word and to the Holy Spirit that they recognize deceit and have the courage to deal with it. Paul's charge to guard the flock from such twisted and distorted influence falls again upon the elders. In such times, plural eldership helps to bear the burden of dealing with false teaching.

Assaults upon the church body and deceit from within the body remind us of a need that we cannot dismiss. The church has always faced grave dangers of false teachers and deceivers luring people from the fold. Elders must stand in the breach against such threats and dangers. If elders were needed nineteen hundred years ago for this task, they are certainly needed today.

SHEPHERDS FOR THE FLOCK (ACTS 20:28, 31)

Acts 20:28, 31 outlines in a straightforward way the duties of elders. While deacons serve in both physical and spiritual realms, the elders are to guard, to keep watch for, and shepherd the church. Because churches face constant threats to doctrinal purity and discipline, elders perform an unceasing role in protecting the church from the adversary's attempts to divide and destroy it.

"Be on guard for yourselves and for all the flock" (Acts 20:28). The concept of being on guard implies that the elders are to "take heed" or "pay attention" to what is being taught, to the trends in the culture, to the actions and behavior in the body so that the church might go forth unhindered in its mission. According to the Scripture text, the guarding actually consists of two elements.

First, elders must guard their own spiritual lives. Elders must personally and as a group give attention to their walks with Christ. They are not to function as ministerial professionals—men who are good at telling others what to do, but who do not practice what they preach. "The mentality of the professional," writes John Piper, "is not the mentality of the prophet. . . . The more professional we long to be, the more spiritual death we will leave in our wake."[11] As John Stott reminds us, "For they cannot care adequately for others if they neglect the care and culture of their own souls."[12]

In Richard Baxter's classic, *The Reformed Pastor,* the chapter titled "The Oversight of Ourselves" identifies a number of things the elder must guard:

1. Take heed to ourselves, lest we should be void of that saving grace of God which we are offering to others.
2. Take heed to ourselves, lest we live with those actual sins which we may preach against in others. Let us see that we are not guilty of that which we may daily condemn.
3. Take heed to ourselves that we may not be unfit for the great tasks

that we have undertaken to complete. We must not be babes in knowledge who will teach men all those mysterious things that are to be known in order to be assured of salvation.

4.   Take heed to ourselves, lest we exemplify contradictory doctrine. Beware, lest we lay such stumbling blocks before the blind that we occasion their ruin. Beware, lest we undo with our lives, what we say with our tongues. Beware, lest we become the greatest hindrance to the success of our own labors.[13]

Second, elders must be on guard for all the flock. Paul uses pastoral terms to express guarding. It is best illustrated by thinking of a group of shepherds gathered on the back of a Judean mountain with their flock of sheep. The sheep munch on the grass and herbs on the mountainside in a rather carefree fashion, while the shepherds constantly watch for thieves who would rob the flock, for wolves that would devour the flock, and for dangers threatening the flock. The job of the shepherd never ends. He constantly watches, constantly checks the health of his flock, constantly ensures that his flock is fed and secure. He knows his sheep and recognizes their needs. An elder operates in a similar fashion, and in addition asks questions of the flock to ascertain their grasp and application of the law and the gospel, and their understanding of justification and sanctification. Fred Malone offers some helpful questions in this regard:

- How does Christ's life and redeeming work help you to live as a husband, a wife, a parent, a child, a church member?
- What do you think is God's great goal for your life?
- What does heaven mean to you today?
- What does Christ think and feel about you when you sin?
- Do you think God enjoys you?[14]

The elders who labor at teaching, preaching, instructing, exhorting, and admonishing the flock fulfill this duty. They must at times reprove those who are in sin. They must admonish those who are toying with compromising the faith. They must instruct and exhort the church to walk in sound doctrine. They must recognize error and not be afraid to address it. Charles Bridges, of the nineteenth century, reminds us that every need in the church body cannot "be fully treated in the pulpit."[15] It requires the individualized attention that can only be given effectively by a plurality of shepherds. Bridges suggests a number of cases that need this kind of special care.

> The indolent are slumbering—the self-dependent are falling back—the zealous are under the influence of spiritual pride—the earnest are becoming self-righteous—the regular, formal. Then there is the enquirer, asking for direction—the tempted and perplexed, looking for support—the afflicted, longing for the cheering consolation of the Gospel—the convinced sinner, from the slight healing of his wound, settling in a delusive peace—the professor, "having a name that he lives; but he is dead." These cases cannot, in all their minute and diversified forms, be fully treated in the pulpit.[16]

Elders must be obedient to the Lord even when implementing difficult decisions. Their concern should never be to conform to popular Christianity so as to gain approval from people in the church. Instead, they should discern biblical Christianity and lead the flock to walk in it without compromise. Elders who aim only for popularity will not care for the flock.

The duty to lead the flock rightly continues with the command, "Be on guard . . . to shepherd the church of God which He purchased with His own blood." Today, we have a rather romantic view of shepherds, especially with Christmas carols referring to them in such glowing terms. But when Paul chose this metaphor to describe the work of elders, he was referring to a job that had no status in society. A shepherd was considered, in fact, the "low-life" of society. The point is clear: the work of shepherding is not for personal fame or reputation, but is to be humble, carried out in loving service as Christ's undershepherd for His flock.

- Shepherding is spiritual work.
- Shepherding is hard work.
- Shepherding is answerable work.

Shepherding is spiritual work. J. Oswald Sanders reminds us, "Spiritual ends can be achieved only by spiritual men who employ spiritual methods."[17] Much is made today of church leaders' being people-pleasers. But truly spiritual men focus on pleasing only one person, the Lord God.

Shepherding is hard work. In Bible times, watching sheep, being constantly on guard for danger, brought on strong mental and emotional strain. Danger was encountered—remember David met a bear and a lion while shepherding. Shepherds trudged across mountains and valleys, through rugged terrain in all weather conditions.

Similarly, the work of elders goes on in all conditions and situations. Elders are never off-duty when they leave the church building. An elder must attend to his own spiritual life, guarding his own family from spiritual dangers. He must maintain a godly example for the rest of the church. While others are resting, he will often be toiling on behalf of the church through study, prayer, ministry, counseling, visiting, and watching.

Shepherding is answerable work. In the apostle Paul's time, shepherds typically worked for someone else. They had the responsibility of giving an account of each sheep before the owner of the flock. Paul reminds the Ephesian elders of this accountability when he tells them "to shepherd the church of God, which He purchased with His own blood." All of us must be reminded that the church does not belong to us. The church belongs to God through the redemptive price of the blood of Christ. We who serve are merely undershepherds who will one day render an account for our duties with God's flock (Heb. 13:17).

John Murray offers a fourfold challenge on what it means to "shepherd the church of God":

1. A shepherd keeps his flock from going astray. In practice this means instruction and warning. . . .
2. A shepherd goes after his sheep when they go astray. In practice this means reproof and correction, in many cases the exercise of ecclesiastical discipline. . . .
3. A shepherd protects his sheep from their enemies. . . . Perhaps there is no more ominous feature of members of the church than the lack of discernment; . . . here the elders in tending the flock must cultivate for themselves and inculcate in the members of

the church, that sensitivity to truth and right, so that they and the people will be able to detect the voice of the enemy. . . .
4. A shepherd leads his flock to the fold; he pours oil into their wounds and gives them pure water to quench their thirst. I would like to press home the necessity and the blessing of the ministry of consolation.[18]

"Therefore be on the alert, remembering that night and day for a period of three years I did not cease to admonish each one with tears" (Acts 20:31). Elders are involved in spiritual warfare—and the church is a battleground! They are called to be alert constantly. Thus, the Word commands elders to stay awake, be continually watchful for those things that would harm the flock. We face the constant opposition of the adversary, who seeks to divide and destroy us at every turn. The Devil is an opportunist looking for those times when our guards are down and our tolerance levels are high. It is at those times he strikes. Consequently, elders must stay at their posts, ever vigilant on behalf of the flock of God.

Paul exemplified vigilance, for three years in that church serving among them, watching and admonishing them with the compassion of tears. For Paul it was not just a job. It was a ministry or commission given from the Lord, and he took it seriously. This is the call to elders: They must recognize that God has given them a ministry and they must perform that ministry as those caring for God's *own* flock.

Notice that Paul took the time to "admonish each one." Admonition can range from instructing by biblical precepts and principles to warning someone through the truth of God that they are going the way of sin.[19] The word for *admonishing* means to "lay upon the mind" *(noutheton)* or to warn or instruct someone who has gone astray of the dangers of the folly of his sin. This is where elders, by precept and practice, are to impact the church. When elders live the Christian life so that others see the need to walk daily with Christ, the church is influenced. As they proclaim the truth of God so that others grow in understanding and practice of the Christian faith, the church is influenced. As elders admonish, they show more care for a person's soul than for that person's approval, and the church feels the impact.

AN UNFORGETABLE FOUNDATION (ACTS 20:28)

One final reminder in this biblical text bears our attention: "Be on guard for yourselves and for all the flock, *among which the Holy Spirit has made you overseers*" (emphasis added). Although Paul and his missionary partners obviously selected the elders, and although they may have had the approval of the congregation, the foundation of the elders' authority was the Holy Spirit, who had made them elders. "So the oversight is his too, or he could not delegate it to others."[20] Elders' ability to serve the body sprang from the distinct calling and setting apart that the Holy Spirit worked in their lives.

This is indeed a mysterious element in the whole work of selecting elders. A congregation seeks to nominate godly men who are confirmed by the qualifications in the Word. The work of the presbytery[21] is to examine the men and present them to the congregation for approval. Then a church sets them apart in a solemn service of ordination. Yet behind it all is the invisible work of the Holy Spirit. He is the One who will ultimately appoint them to this office in the church. John Stott writes, "This splendid Trinitarian affirmation, that the pastoral oversight of the church belongs to God (Father, Son, and Holy Spirit), should have a profound effect on pastors. It should humble us to remember that the church is not ours, but God's. And it should inspire us to faithfulness."[22]

I confess that I do not understand all of this working of the Holy Spirit. But I am humbled by the truth that the Holy Spirit, who corporately dwells among the church (Eph. 2:22), works to set men apart for the noble work of elders. And because the Holy Spirit does this work, the church must pay heed to the importance of both the exercise of its ministry and its response to the elders' leadership.

The Holy Spirit makes these men to be "overseers" not "overlords." They are not given the role of dictators, but humble, loving servant-leaders in the congregation. They are to exercise their duties in dependence on the same Spirit who set them apart, recognizing that their hands cannot do all that needs to be done in the lives of God's people. They must trust the Holy Spirit to work in the secret places of men's minds and hearts to accomplish the divine task before them.

The dangers we face in twenty-first-century America are of the same nature as those faced by our first-century counterparts. The same Lord who directed the apostles to appoint spiritual leaders over the early church gives clear direction for doing the same in modern churches. When selecting those leaders, popularity must be laid aside and biblical qualifications instead emphasized. Every man nominated by his church must examine himself in light of God's Word before accepting that nomination and the challenge of serving his congregation.

REFLECTIONS

- In what ways does the church at Ephesus resemble your own church?
- What are the primary responsibilities given to the Ephesian elders?
- What part do the elders' spiritual lives play in the overall effectiveness of their work?
- What does Paul mean by guarding and shepherding the church of God? How are these needs being addressed in your own church setting?

CHAPTER FIVE

Elders and Congregation in Concert

Hebrews 13:17–19

I've heard many stories of church conflict. Although such conflicts vary, they find their ultimate root in the leader's failure to lead and/or the congregation's failure to follow. Sometimes leaders attempt to lead and congregations refuse to follow. On other occasions, willing congregations flounder in spiritual inertia because their leaders fail to give biblical leadership. Conflicts naturally ensue. Church leaders—elders, deacons, pastors, staff, teachers—and congregations must be diligent in understanding and following the biblical patterns for church life. The relationship of leaders and congregations, in truth, really sets the tone for spiritual growth and development. The epistle to the Hebrews offers an example of this truth.

Hebrews is, in fact, a massive doctrinal epistle. For depth, richness, clarity, and forcefulness in explaining Christ and the gospel, the content of Hebrews rivals that of any portion of Holy Writ. Yet with all of its doctrinal depth, Hebrews remains one of the Bible's most practical books. Its pastoral implications shine throughout the epistle. Philip E. Hughes, after identifying many in today's church who satisfy themselves with "an undemanding and superficial association with the Christian faith," explains that the letter to the Hebrews was written "to arouse just such persons from the lethargic state of compromise and complacency into which they had sunk, and to incite them to persevere wholeheartedly in the Christian conflict." He adds, "[Hebrews] is a tonic for the spiritually debilitated."[1] The writer, "clearly a preacher with a pastoral heart,"[2] had no desire to launch into minutiae; rather, he sought to bring a congregation of believers into a steady, focused, and persevering walk with Jesus Christ. "The writer of Hebrews," writes Andrew Trotter Jr., "shows that combination of toughness and tenderness that is so crucial in ministry. Even when his warnings are as stringent as any in the NT, he makes sure to encourage those whom he believes are on the right track."[3]

It is not surprising, then, that in an epistle of such strong doctrinal language the pastoral writer would address the critical relationship between the congregation—or at least some of its members—and its present leaders. Disjointed relations in this setting could unravel the Christ-centered argument that the writer sets forth in the epistle, and which the church's leadership would seek to engage and apply. Since "this author knows his readers intimately,"[4] he left no stone unturned that might hinder their full application of the doctrine of Christ to their lives. An unwillingness to follow their spiritual leaders posed such a danger.

Nothing in Hebrews indicates that the elders and teachers in this particular church had forsaken their responsibilities. Despite their faithfulness, though, some of the congregation had balked at following them. Accordingly, the writer of Hebrews exhorts the congregation to remember the spiritual leaders who had already passed from the scene, and imitate their faith (13:7). With regard to current leaders, the pastoral writer charges the congregation to follow its spiritual leadership (13:17). Both of these exhortations (vv. 7, 17) indicate the connection between the doctrine set forth and its application in daily walk.

Trotter conjectures that the epistle is actually addressed to "a small group of former leaders in the church [who] have encountered difficulties submitting to the current leadership."[5] Perhaps they had suffered under the bloodless persecutions of Claudius in A.D. 49, and the vicious, bloody persecutions of Nero a few years later. Having undergone the trauma of ill treatment due to their faith, they felt shell-shocked once they surfaced and came back into active church life. The keenness of their doctrine had begun to fray, and so had their loyalty to those presently leading the church. So the pastoral writer of Hebrews firmly corrects their theological errors, warns of the dangers of returning to the legalism of Judaism, and rebukes their lapse in following the leaders in the church.[6]

The string of pointed applications in the last chapter of Hebrews serves to reinforce that doctrine is always applicable to daily life. Any congregation's spiritual leaders should major on helping the church to apply the teaching of God's Word. *As leaders are to lead the church in applying truth to life, even so the congregations are to follow.* But how does this flesh out in the ongoing life of the church? Hebrews 13:17–19 might best be investigated under two headings.

Hebrews 13:17–19
- Leaders Who Lead (vv. 17–18)
- Congregations That Follow (vv. 17–19)

LEADERS WHO LEAD (HEB. 13:17–18)

It is true that Hebrews 13:17–18 does not mention the titles *elder, overseer,* or *pastor.* Yet the term used, *leaders,* clearly points to the biblical office of elder. *Leaders* is actually a participle that can be translated, "the ones leading you," demonstrating plural leadership (eldership) in this congregation. The word is used similarly in Luke 22:26; Acts 14:12; and 15:22.[7] Whether this particular congregation called its "leaders" *elders, overseers,* or *pastors,* they were, in fact, involved in governing, teaching, and shepherding the church—the very functions of plural eldership.

While today we have no shortage of books, principles, and seminars on leadership, we do have a shortage of godly leaders. Every church needs a plurality of men who will faithfully exemplify the Christian life and clearly articulate the teachings of Scripture as they take care of the individual flocks that make up the church of the Lord Jesus Christ. What are leaders to be doing? While Hebrews is by no means exhaustive, it is helpful in directing leaders in how to lead.

Watchfulness

Hebrews 13:17 set forth a reminder that spiritual leaders have the incredible demand of keeping watch over the church: "For they keep watch over your souls as those who will give an account." The word translated *keep watch* is a strong one,[8] picturing a shepherd who keeps careful and sacrificial vigilance over his flock. The shepherd's concern to protect the flock from wolves that would snatch the sheep cause him to go without sleep and to strain at discerning any cause of trouble. Watchfulness also has a military connotation—that of soldiers guarding their post, keeping vigilant lest the enemy sneak in to cause harm. Such careful watchfulness is to be "over your souls," which is another way of expressing that the leaders' concern is to be for the whole person, or for "the seat and center of life that transcends the earthly."[9]

Spiritual leaders must maintain an alertness and discernment in attending to their duties with the church. Their duties chiefly focus on the people who make up the church rather than on buildings or budgets. What kinds of things are they to watch on behalf of (*over* is better translated, "on behalf of") the church? *First, they are to watch for dangerous doctrines and false teaching.* This is the clear example of the apostle Paul to the church at Ephesus: "Be on guard for yourselves and for all the flock, among which the Holy Spirit has made you overseers, to shepherd the church of God which He purchased with His own blood. I know that after my departure savage wolves will come in among you, not sparing the flock; and from among your own selves men will arise, speaking perverse things, to draw away the disciples after them. Therefore be on the alert" (Acts 20:28–31). Spiritual leaders need to keep their fingers on the pulse of doctrine and teaching in a church. Surely, more heresies, half-truths, and pseudodoctrines than we can imagine are being passed off as truth.

A few years ago my family attended a Baptist church in Atlanta while visiting with relatives. The pastor read the Scripture and said, "May God bless His Spirit-inspired Word so that it *becomes the Word of God to us today*" (emphasis added). That was right out of the pages of neo-orthodox theology that denies the full authority of Scripture. It does not *become* the Word of God; it *is* the Word of God. The congregation was duped by this man's charisma in the pulpit. They needed some spiritual leaders who could discern such slick teaching and address it biblically.

Perhaps even more dangerous is the disappearance of theology in evangelical churches while spiritual leaders—in dereliction of their duties—ignore that it is happening. David Wells has pointed out, "No one has abducted theology," as in the abduction of a child. Rather, "The disappearance is closer to what happens in homes where the children are ignored and, to all intents and purposes, abandoned. They remain in the home, but they have no place in the family. So it is with theology in the church. It remains on the edges of evangelical life, but it has been dislodged from its center."[10] Watchfulness of a congregation demands attentiveness to the church's theological understanding. Neglect of theology cracks the church's foundation, and ultimately affects its practice. In our day, one of the chief results of such neglect is the rise of pragmatism, which has moved the church away from a biblically centered ministry that effectively changes the church to a church structure that more resembles the world than the New Testament pattern.[11] Wells adds, "It is evangelical *practice* rather than evangelical profession that reveals the change."[12] As evangelicals, we still profess to believe the confessions and creeds of the church, but our practice reveals that we often do not understand the theological implications of what we profess. Spiritual leaders must remain alert and watchful for this kind of neglect.

Add to this the countless false teachers on the airwaves and the cult groups that masquerade as Christian, and spiritual leaders clearly need to be on full-time alert due to the dangers facing the church. "Savage wolves" were not just a first-century phenomenon. Marauding packs continue to ravage churches, using dangerous doctrines and false teaching. Spiritual leaders must stand in the breach against such error foisted on the church.

Second, spiritual leaders must keep on the alert for deceitful behavior within the church. Tucked away in the little epistle of 3 John is the warning about Diotrephes, who had grabbed the leadership reigns of a church as a dictator. D. Edmund Hiebert describes him as "an ambitious, self-seeking, power-hungry individual who aggressively sought to be at the head of things and to rule over others."[13] While he might have masked his motives with orthodox words, he was actually self-centered and full of pride, seeking to use the church to fulfill his own lust for power. The apostle John exposed his deceitful behavior and calls on the church to resist such wickedness (3 John 9–10). Here, John gives a clear example of the work of church elders. Deceitful behavior must be exposed before it wrecks the church.

Recently, I have been involved in ministering to a fellow pastor who had a couple of men like Diotrephes in his church. Although he sought to address the problems nobly and biblically, he recognized that the spiritual leaders of the church failed to expose these deceitful men that grabbed for the reins of power. Asleep on the job, the church's spiritual leaders allowed the wolves to freely ravage the church and undermine the pastor's ministry. The failure of this church to reflect the beauty of Christ in the community must be traced back ultimately to the spiritual leaders' abrogation of their responsibilities to remain alert to deceitful behavior in the church.

Third, spiritual leaders must keep alert to divisive behaviors. Wouldn't it be wonderful if we could make a wish, and watch all divisiveness in churches blow away? But that is not reality. We will always face that battle in the church of Jesus Christ. Spiritual leaders have the responsibility to stand firmly against divisiveness—by rebuking, admonishing, and even leading the way in exercising discipline leaders arrest such rending of the church. "Reject a factious man after a first and second warning, knowing that such a man is perverted and is sinning, being self-condemned," Paul instructed Titus (Titus 3:10–11). None of these things are popular measures in a church. But it is the lot of spiritual leaders—the elders—who would "keep watch over your souls." P. H. Mell identifies divisive behaviors as one of several "public offenses" in which the sin is "against the Church in its organized capacity."[14] In other words, not merely one member is offended, but the entire church is affected by divisiveness. Spiritual leaders watching over the souls of the church dare not hesitate in applying disciplinary measures against offenders. The health and unity of the church is at stake.

Fourth, spiritual leaders must keep alert to the church's spiritual development. This includes the positive aspect of knowing, teaching, and encouraging spiritual growth in the church. Paying attention to the content offered the church in times of instruction, and how members respond, gives the elders a better grasp of the church's maturity and ability to discern false teaching.[15]

Accountability

As a pastor and elder in my own congregation, I find no thought more alarming than the one found in this verse: "For they keep watch over your souls *as those who will give an account*" (emphasis added). Church leaders will give an account of their ministry to the church—an awesome realization for those who take seriously their leadership charge. Leaders must never forget that a portion of the body of Christ expects faithfulness and diligence in the duties that have been given to those leaders. As a pastor, I sense this accountability. My own church does not take lightly the work of ministry—and never should. The church needs to maintain high expectations in regard to elders, in terms of personal walk with Christ, ministering the Word, and setting an example for the body.

But the accountability spoken of in this passage points to another day—the great day of accounting when we all stand before the Lord in judgment. Just as James explains that teachers "will incur stricter judgment," spiritual leaders will be required to give an account of how they discharged their responsibilities as shepherds of the flock of God (James 3:1; 1 Peter 4:5). The same word for *accounting* is used in 1 Peter 4:5 when Peter speaks of judgment, and the accounting that will be given by all men. But here it pointedly reveals more intense scrutiny by the eye that sees all and the mind that knows all. This is why Paul prefaced his exhortation to Timothy to "preach the word" by reminding him, "I solemnly charge you in the presence of God and of Christ Jesus, who is to judge the living and the dead" (2 Tim. 4:1). "In the presence of God" is more literally rendered, "in the face of God." Because the relationship of doctrine and practice is tied so closely to the leadership of those in charge of God's flock, the Lord alerts His undershepherds that a time of accounting will take place.

This accounting faces all the spiritual leaders in the church, who must remember that when our day is done, we will give an account for the discharge of our responsibilities in the church. So we are reminded to live and serve as those who will answer to the Lord of the church for our ministries. "This solemn consideration should affect not only the quality of their leadership," writes Philip Hughes, "but also the quality of the obedience with which the Christian community responds to that leadership."[16] The sobering reality of eternity should never slip beyond the sight of spiritual leaders and their congregations.

Seriousness

Great seriousness, then, accompanies spiritual leadership. There is more to holding the office than simply wearing a title of *pastor, elder,* or *deacon.* It calls for serving in good conscience and with due diligence.

Evidently, charges had been made against or rumors circulated about the writer of Hebrews. Some had attacked him, perhaps as viciously as the Corinthians and Galatians had Paul, charging that he had been a slacker or that he was out for personal gain or that he was poor in his leadership. We can only guess the charges, but we do see his quiet response: "For we are sure that we have a good conscience" (Heb. 13:18). That would have been an odd statement unless the writer was responding to charges leveled against him. He sees no need to give a lengthy explanation. His epistle has certainly verified the excellence of his grasp of God's Word, his love for the gospel, and his passion for this congregation's spiritual growth. So he needed only to affirm, "For we are sure that we have a good conscience," meaning, as Hughes explains, "that his conduct in relation to them can stand the scrutiny both of man and of God."[17] *We* is called an epistolary pronoun, which means that *We* served as a substitute for *I.* Lest we think that he was boasting he quickly asserts his desire to be honorable in his Christian ethics: "desiring to conduct ourselves honorably in all things." It was not a confession of having arrived spiritually, but one that affirmed this pastor's seriousness in exercising his ministry. Surely he models the conduct still needed by those holding the offices of spiritual leaders in local churches.

Consider one other note about the seriousness of leadership. In the second sentence of 13:17, the writer says, "Let them do this with joy and not with grief, for this would be unprofitable for you." Christian leadership is not without emotion. *Joy* and *grief* are two very different terms that characterize the emotional response to the demands upon Christian leaders. *Let them do this* (a present subjunctive verb that takes on a hortatory sense) commands action on the part of the church.[18] They were not to respond to the leadership with neutrality; rather, they were to respond so that their leaders might carry out their duties "with joy and not with grief." Leaders cannot find joy or grief unless they take their responsibilities seriously. Joy comes when the leader senses that Christ is being formed in the church (Gal. 4:19), while grief results in seeing either rebellion against the Word or apathy toward spiritual disciplines.

Conduct

The only way that leaders will feel the weight of accountability in their offices is when considering their own conduct. As they first guard their own hearts they will be prepared to watch over God's flock. If they know that a day of accounting will come before the Chief Shepherd, out of that knowledge should flow a desire to guard their conduct. If they take their charge seriously, then their lives serve as a model for the flock (Heb. 13:7). Hence the plea for prayer is given—"Pray for us"—and the reason—"desiring to conduct ourselves honorably in all things" (v. 18). *Desiring* intensely expresses the deepest wish and longing of the spiritual leader's heart. Leaders know that they and the congregation they serve are sinners, in constant need of grace. They know that they cannot just preach and teach and implore others while neglecting their own conduct. They know that they have weaknesses that the adversary would gladly exploit through multiplied temptations.[19] They know that they grow tired and weary, and at times consider throwing off the yoke of spiritual leadership for lesser accountability. And so, knowing all this, the writer of Hebrews urges the church to pray for him that his deepest longing of honorable conduct "in all things" might be fulfilled.

When all is said and done, though a spiritual leader may not be a great preacher or teacher, may fall short in administrative skills, may falter in his abilities to counsel, and may lack stamina for his duties, *he must not dishonor the noble office entrusted to him by the church through failing in his conduct.* Other things are important, but the spiritual leader's conduct as a Christian serves as the foundation for the whole of his ministry. Neglect his conduct, and his ministry is negated. But honor the Lord in his conduct and, even with weaknesses, he will prove to be faithful.

CONGREGATIONS THAT FOLLOW (HEB. 13:17–19)

Faithful leaders must also have faithful congregations, or else their whole labor will be "with grief" rather than with joy. Observers often consider the church nothing more than a social organization with religious overtones. Even some among local congregations might think of the church only in business and organizational management terms. Yet the Scripture holds a different viewpoint. The writer of Hebrews exhorted his readers not to forsake their regular assembling together. He viewed the church as "brethren," united in one family of believers with each bearing responsibility for encouraging one another, and motivating "one another to love and good deeds." Because the church has access into God's presence through "the blood of Jesus," looking to Christ as "a great high priest over the house of God," then the church is to unite in drawing near to God as a praying people, in standing together upon their common confession of Christ, and in mutual care and fellowship with one another (Heb. 10:19–25). The church "alone enjoys this freedom of access" into God's holy presence as regenerate people.[20] The church holds firmly its confession of Christ, "first publicly made at their baptism, but also a witness thereafter to be joyfully maintained to the very end of this life."[21] The church cannot exist with "selfish individualism," which is the breeding ground for division.[22] Instead, the individual members of the church must look for ways to incite one another in the practices that characterize true believers.[23] And this certainly cannot take place by absenteeism from the church's stated gatherings for the study of God's Word, worship, and service.

In every age, the church's greatest threats come in the areas of "doctrine and life, or belief and behavior," as Philip Ryken explains. "The rebellion of the mind is to deny what God tells us to think (which today takes the form of relativism)."[24] That's why the writer of Hebrews exhorts the church to "hold fast the confession of our hope without wavering" (Heb. 10:23). Ryken continues, "The rebellion of the heart is to disobey what God commands us to do (which today takes the form of narcissism)."[25] And that is why the church must be constantly engaged in inciting "one another to love and good deeds." Yet how can this take place in the realm of practice? The New Testament clearly shows that "God's plan was to place the church under the care of shepherds."[26] Shepherds lead while the membership of the church follows this God-given leadership in doctrine and practice.

Obedience and Submission

Perhaps the most difficult part of this text is found in the opening words of Hebrews 13:17: "Obey your leaders and submit to them, for they keep watch over your souls as those who will give an account." The words *obey* and *submit* conjure thoughts of a wicked slave owner, cracking a whip to bring his slaves under servile obedience. But that is foreign to the idea of this text. A closer look at the text reveals the responsibility that God has given to each one in the church.

Spiritual leaders have the responsibility of keeping watch "over your souls," that is, on behalf of your life. God has given protection to the church. He does not desire anyone in the church to stumble by false teaching or enticement to sin or the allurements of the world. He has given us ample warnings of all these things in His Word. He has given us the holy example of our Lord as well as that of the apostles and believers through the centuries (cf. Heb. 11:1–12:1–3). But in the great mercy of God, He has placed spiritual leaders—elders—among the church who have the responsibility to be vigilant in recognizing and dealing with spiritual hindrances.

When, for instance, a false teaching arises among the churches, the elders are to stand against it for the sake of the flock whom they serve. Using God's Word, they are to prove that error is being foisted upon unsuspecting Christians. They are to expose such error, warn of its danger, and seek to keep the church out of *spiritual harm's way*. It is unfortunate that this ministry by spiritual leaders is often taken too lightly by their congregation or left to the work of a single pastor. Does the church know the vigilance that is required just to *recognize* false teaching? Do they understand the agony that is involved in trying to deal with error, often in the face of misunderstanding and opposition? Ryken explains, "Elders and pastors are called to master biblical theology, to spend time studying God's Word and learning the great doctrines of the Christian faith."[27] They risk offending others while standing for the truth. They face misunderstanding while seeking to correct those in error. Often they are subjected to ridicule by the world and even some within the church, all for the sake of the congregation given to their charge.

How is the church to respond to those who "keep watch over your souls"? The congregation can obey and submit, or it can stiffen and rebel. There is no middle ground, for apathy is simply quiet rebellion. If you see the value of spiritual leadership and you recognize that God has placed that leadership in the church for your benefit, then the only response is to obey and submit to such spiritual leaders. Those rebelling commit spiritual anarchy. John Chrysostom, the "Golden-tongued preacher" of the fourth century wrote, "Anarchy is an evil, the occasion of many calamities, and the source of disorder and confusion"; moreover, "a people that does not obey a ruler [i.e., elder or pastor] is like one that has none, and perhaps even worse."[28] But the individualism and narcissism characterizing much of the church reacts to the call for obedience and submission. In spite of how unpopular it might be, however, the Lord of the church determined that His body function with plural leaders—to guard against abuse—and faithful members who value obedience and submission as a joyful responsibility.

Both *obey* and *submit* are present imperatives, showing constancy on the part of the church. The obedience called for does not imply becoming "man-followers" rather than followers of Christ. Following Christ remains the church's priority; we are to follow spiritual leadership *only* as it imitates Christ and adheres to the teaching of the Word. We are never to obey and submit in areas that are clearly in conflict with the teaching of Scripture.

Some use these verses to claim *absolute authority,* but that belongs only to the Lord. A simple rule of thumb is that "sanctified common sense" must be used in obeying and submitting to spiritual leaders. These verses command obedience and submission in the realm of the church and the spiritual life. They do not imply that spiritual leaders have authority to dictate the membership's personal affairs as relates to finances, business decisions, and even marriage partners. Certainly they can offer counsel in these areas, and may even exhort church members in godly wisdom, but never control. "They keep watch over your souls," not your bank accounts.[29]

Spiritual leaders bear responsibility for speaking the Word of God to the congregation and giving it an example to follow. In this context we can see the need to obey and submit. *Obey* carries the idea of obediently following someone because you trust that person. The implication is that the church hears the elders' teaching of the Word and sees their seriousness in following the teaching of Scripture, so they obediently do likewise. An elder should never adopt an attitude that commands "do as I say not as I do." Elders are to set the example so that the writer of Hebrews can confidently say, "Imitate their faith" (Heb. 13:7).

Submit recognizes the God-ordained authority established in the church for order and direction. The congregation submits or places itself under the leadership of its spiritual leaders, complying with their direction and teaching. "If obedience applies to the leaders' teaching, then submission relates to their leaders' function."[30] Raymond Brown offers a needed clarification on what submission means.

> One of the markedly unhealthy aspects of some contemporary teaching is the current "shepherding" fashion and the notion, popularized in some house churches and elsewhere, that every believer is meant to have a spiritual mentor to whom he is fully accountable for every aspect of his life. The spiritual "elder" has to be consulted before making significant purchases, changing one's job and accepting fresh responsibilities. The Scripture does not teach, encourage, or exemplify submission of this sort. It is bad for the one who practises *[sic]* it in that it discourages personal accountability to the Lord God, a mark of true Christian maturity. Furthermore, it minimizes the importance of other deep relationships, especially marriage, through which the will of God can be most naturally discerned.[31]

Our lives are best regulated and governed when we walk in submission to the authority that God has placed in our lives. In the church, that authority is found in those whom God raises up as spiritual leaders. "Submission to authority is absolutely necessary for the proper ordering of society, and the church of God is no exception. Indeed, submission to authority is often a test of our submission to God."[32] So *obey* and *submit* are not offensive orders, but terms for orderly life in the church.

Profit or Loss?

Hebrews 13:17 ends with an earnest plea: "Let them do this with joy and not with grief, for this would be unprofitable for you." Elders face weighty responsibilities and demands. They are to give leadership to the congregation in the ways of God. They are to teach and exhort the congregation in the doctrines of God's Word. They are to live exemplary lives, serving as living models of the Christian faith to the congregation. And they are to constantly watch over the souls in the congregation, guarding them from deceit, error, sin, and worldliness. In light of all this, the responsibility of the church is to "let them do this with joy and not with grief."

Elders and deacons are to find their greatest delights in carrying out their weighty responsibilities with their church. It is to be a joy to lead, teach, give example, and watch over souls. They are to constantly look forward to each day's challenge in spiritual leadership. John MacArthur writes,

> It is the responsibility of the church to help their leaders rule with joy and satisfaction. One way of doing this is through willing submission to their authority. The joy of our leaders in the Lord should be a motivation for submission. We are not to submit begrudgingly or out of a feeling of compulsion, but willingly, so that our elders and pastors may experience joy in their work with us.[33]

A humble attitude in the members of the congregation is essential if elders are to experience joy in their duties. If someone in the congregation demonstrates jealousy of those who are in positions of spiritual leadership, that attitude will greatly reduce the joy of the spiritual leaders. Those who are resentful about being under the authority of another in the ministry of the church create division and strife within the congregation. A world of trouble results when church members rebel against this clear teaching of Scripture.

"Let them do this with joy"—so what is the "this" of the text? It is specifically that all-encompassing work of keeping watch over the congregation's souls. Members contribute to the overall effectiveness of this work by their attitudes toward those whom God has placed as leaders in the body. "Grief" or "groaning," caused by callousness to the Word and arrogance toward spiritual leadership, would be unprofitable for the church. Brown adds, "If spiritual leaders have to labour [sic] under grim and hostile conditions in the local church, then that does not work out to the members' immediate good and certainly not to their ultimate advantage."[34]

But the joy of which Hebrews speaks is not one-sided. The text continues, pointing out that to neglect obedience and submission to leaders "would be unprofitable for you." The Greek word for *unprofitable* literally means "harmful" for you.[35] The plural pronoun *you* clearly refers to the church. The whole church, then, will find it harmful when even a few are rebelling against the spiritual leadership of the church.

Why is this so? As the church, we are mysteriously woven together in the bonds of Jesus Christ. Every local church is unique in being a visible expression of the body of Christ. Every church becomes a family of believers who must learn to live with each other, labor with each other, learn with each other, and face adversities with each other. When one is joyful all are to be joyful. When one is grieving all share in that grief. By that same rule, however, one person's attitude affects the whole church. When someone in the church rebels against or even becomes secretly agitated toward spiritual leadership of the church, the whole body is affected.

Urgency in Prayer

In light of all the responsibilities given to spiritual leaders and the congregation, the pastor who is the author of Hebrews asks his readers to pray for him and the other spiritual leaders in the church. "Pray for us," he implores, so that they might conduct themselves honorably as Christians, elders, and leaders. Then he adds a note of urgency: "And I urge you all the more to do this, so that I may be restored to you the sooner" (Heb. 13:19). We do not know what hindered the writer from returning to this church, over which he had assigned spiritual leadership. A short time later, he states that Timothy had been released, presumably from prison, and that the writer planned to come with Timothy. Whatever the hindrance, the writer understood that overcoming it would require God's intervention. He needed the prayers of this congregation in order to live honorably before the Lord and to be positioned to fulfill his responsibilities to the church. So as they pray for his return, the church must obey and submit to the other leaders in the church.

Simply put, then, not only does the church need spiritual leaders, but spiritual leaders also need the church and its prayers. Kent Hughes states this clearly from his years of Christian service.

> How different the modern church would be if the majority of its people prayed for its pastors and lay leadership. There would be supernatural suspensions of business-as-usual worship. There would be times of inexplicable visitations from the Holy Spirit. More laypeople would come to grips with the deeper issues of life. The leadership vacuum would evaporate. There would be more conversions.[36]

As a pastor and elder, my particular needs might be different from those of the other elders and leaders in our church, but the need for the prayers of God's people who are called South Woods Baptist Church (my own congregation) remains paramount. Without their faithful praying our ministry will not succeed. But with it, there is no limit to what our gracious God might be pleased to do through our congregation. So, joining with my first-century counterpart, I urge you to pray for the leaders of your own congregation. Pray for their Christian walks and discipline. Pray for their roles as husbands and fathers. Pray for their grasp and understanding of the Word. Pray for their preaching and teaching the Word. Pray for the times of counseling and witnessing, as well as for the times of direction and decision-making in which they engage. Pray, that in the end we might all serve Christ together with joy to His glory alone!

REFLECTIONS

- What does the writer of Hebrews teach concerning what spiritual leaders are to be doing on behalf of the church?
- How are spiritual leaders held accountable?
- How should the church respond to its spiritual leaders?
- In what ways are spiritual leaders dependent on the church?

CHAPTER SIX

Spiritual Leaders for God's Flock

1 Peter 5:1–5

Elders is admittedly an alien term in Baptist life. Although other denominations frequently use the term, Baptists rarely do. On those rare occasions, Baptists usually redefine elders as "church staff." But does this do justice to the biblical term?

During most of the nineteenth and twentieth centuries, elders fell out of normal Baptist structure and church life. Mark Dever suggests that the change in structure may have been caused by either the neglect of biblical teaching or to the rapid spread of the church into the frontier regions of our nation. With so many churches started so quickly, the local leadership may have been hampered in forming a plurality of elders.[1] The growth of Baptists by 1844 "represented an increase of 360 per cent in thirty years," while the population increase of the nation was only 140 percent in the same period.[2] Much of the growth took place in rural and frontier areas, under untrained ministers planting churches among a people imbued with individualistic and democratic ideologies in the wake of the American Revolution.[3] The Baptist emphasis on congregationalism, combined with the early American emphasis on individualism, likely resulted in the decline of churches being governed through elder plurality. Additionally, with the move into the frontier, the "one elder" structure of a pastor, who often served several churches, was a necessity of last resort rather than biblical conviction. Dever explains, "Elders could be found in Baptist churches in America throughout the eighteenth century and into the nineteenth century."[4] But our century is different.

It can be observed, however, as Daryl Cornett points out, during this era, elder plurality was not uncommon with some Baptist churches. "These congregations viewed the elders as equal in their office but different in their duties. Some were charged with pastoral duties and some with administrative duties of the church." Yet the ultimate authority in these churches still "resided in the congregation corporately."[5]

Some Baptists in the nineteenth century continued the practice of elder plurality. A leading voice among them was W. B. Johnson, the first president of the Southern Baptist Convention. Preferring the term *bishop*, since it conveyed the idea of overseeing a congregation in its spiritual life, Johnson stated in 1846, "A plurality in the bishopric is of great importance for mutual counsel and aid, that the government and edification of the flock may be promoted in the best manner."[6] He explained that, with a plurality, all elders would maintain a sense of equality in position, but each would offer to the church different gifts and ministry. In this respect the church would receive the kind of ministry necessary for its ongoing health.

Standing on the same tradition of some of the previous centuries' Baptists, our own church adopted what I would call a "modified congregational/elder structure of church government." We still have the basic elements of congregational rule familiar to Baptist life through the past four hundred years. We differ from our friends in the Presbyterian General Assembly and Bible Churches who put final authority in the hands of the local session of elders or submit to a presbytery outside of the local church. In contrast, the final authority on matters of our church life resides in the congregation. But the functioning of a purely congregational system is both unwieldy and lacking biblical support. Instead, the establishment of a body of elders to serve in day-to-day leadership in spiritual matters, serving at the pleasure of the congregation, enables us to maintain both the traditional distinctive of congregational life and the clearly biblical structure of elders.

The New Testament does not hand local churches a concretely formed structure for governance. While cookie-cutter polity had no place in the early church, the Bible does offer an outline or skeleton for the structuring of churches. As has been noted, this can easily be traced through the book of Acts as the church emerges. The apostles exercised all leadership authority in the beginning. This changed, however, when the problem arose of the Hellenistic widows missing out on food distribution. Solving this problem led to the creation of a group of "servants" that could minister to the widows' needs. This set the stage for the development of church polity (Acts 6:1–7). In one sense it can be affirmed that church polity was reactive rather than strictly proactive. New needs arose and, in response to those needs the structure developed over a period of time. The church enlarged into new regions far beyond the oversight of the apostles, so local church leadership proved essential. Once the dust of years settled, the church recognized elders and deacons as those called to serve the body's spiritual and temporal needs, and to maintain a course of faithfulness.

All details, however, of the functioning of the church are not laid out for us. Culture, timeframes, and needs determine the extent of how such a structure is fleshed out. Yet the basic structure must be present as the backbone for healthy New Testament churches. Critical to this structure is the establishment of a group of spiritual leaders called elders, overseers, or pastors.

A church's insistence on strong spiritual leadership adds stability, unity, and health to the congregation. Far too often, local churches leave spiritual leadership to chance. Church polity is rarely evaluated in light of Scripture; church leadership seldom meets biblical standards. Pastors are called, staffs are hired, deacons are elected, and everything is business as usual. Church business meetings typically expose raw nerves and power struggles. Unqualified leaders and unwieldy structures foment church disunity. In an effort to deflect problems created by an eroded foundation, staff changes are made and new programs added, with the hope that the accompanying fanfare will pump new life into a decaying structure. A new crop of even younger deacons is elected to infuse fresh blood into a deathly anemic organism. This cycle occurs again and again, developing only frustration and disappointment, never strong churches.

But there is a better way, a courageous way of returning to the biblical patterns of church life. At the heart of a church's development is its spiritual leadership. If the leadership lacks the character needed for such holy work, the character of the church will be lacking, too. Instability will result if the church is not structured according to biblical principles and patterns. Short-term solutions of new programs and new ideas do not solve long-term problems with character and stability. Only by returning to the biblical model for church structure and life can the church confidently press on in a world that is becoming increasingly hostile to biblical Christianity. It is true that developing an elder leadership structure will not solve every problem. But such a reorienting toward the biblical pattern and principles establishes a framework for developing strong and healthy churches. How, though, do elders fit into the fabric of congregational life? The investigation of this subject focuses on three questions.

---

1 Peter 5:1–5

- How Are Spiritual Leaders Identified? (vv. 1–2)
- How Do Elders and the Congregation Function? (vv. 2–5)
- Who Holds the Elders Accountable? (v. 4)

HOW ARE SPIRITUAL LEADERS IDENTIFIED? (1 PETER 5:1–2)

The context of 1 Peter 5 helps in grasping the importance of elders in everyday church life. Just before explaining the ministry of elders, Peter addressed the subject of suffering for the sake of the gospel, calling it "the fiery ordeal among you, which comes upon you for your testing" (4:12; see also vv. 13–19). Robert Leighton noted that in the "fiery ordeal" the early Christians faced, "there is an accession of troubles and hatreds for that holiness of life to which the children of God are called."[7] Persecution seemed to be the common lot of these believers in Asia Minor. Christianity's association with Judaism subjected it to Roman intolerance for the refusal of both to participate in some of the empire's religious practices. Because Christianity was a non-Roman religion, it may have been under the suspicion of the Roman officials who feared the proliferation of non-sanctioned organizations—which in their minds might pose a political threat to Roman authority. Some of the provinces, particularly Asia Minor, showed their loyalty to the emperor through paying him divine honors. Christians abhorred this kind of practice, and refusal to cooperate likely caused local officials to pressure them into conformity, with resulting persecution. Ultimately, "Christians faced what was perhaps an even greater threat from the attitudes of the general populace."[8] This might have come through accusations that Christians lived immoral lives, so Peter counters this by exhorting them to "keep a good conscience so that in the thing in which you are slandered, those who revile your good behavior in Christ will be put to shame" (3:16). Refusal to participate in local superstitious practices probably led to charges of disloyalty to the government, so Peter exhorts the believers to submit to the governing authorities, "that by doing right you may silence the ignorance of foolish men" (2:15; see also vv. 13–14). Since the Christians kept themselves from some of the social engagements that aligned with idolatrous practices, others in the community would have accused them of aloofness. Accusations led to estrangement and opposition. Believers suffered for the sake of the gospel.[9]

The theme of suffering continues after the portion dealing with elders (5:1–5), as Peter again deals with the suffering that Christians face, via both the anxieties of life and the attacks of the Devil (5:6–11). His discussion of elders comes in the middle of his exhortation to persevere during suffering. How are these matters critically related? If these believers were to face times of suffering with a sense of dignity and dependence on the Lord, they needed the nurturing and example that would come by way of the church elders. The author of Hebrews perceived the same thing (Heb. 13:7). Elders were never to replace the spiritual life of the congregation, but were to enhance it through their faithful instruction and application of God's Word to the church. They were to provide tangible models for the church—"proving to be examples to the flock"—in the face of life's difficulties.

By Position

We must identify the position within congregational life that Peter addresses. Notice how Peter tells his readers *I'm one of you:* "Therefore, I exhort the elders among you, as your fellow elder." It is obvious that he is not referring simply to the older men in the congregation since he identifies their having been given oversight of God's flock, and additionally, they were to refrain from using their position to lord it over the ones under their charge.[10]

As noted previously, the term *elders* was common in Jewish life, referring to leaders in Israel or those blessed of God with advanced years. Due to their maturity they were given responsibilities for leading their communities. The Greek counterpart for this term is *overseer* or *bishop*, referring to those leaders in the city-states who had responsibilities for exercising administrative oversight under the emperor's command. The third New Testament term used synonymously with *elder* is *pastor*. The word emphasizes the role of caring for, feeding, leading, and providing for the flock. Acts 20:17–35 and Peter's text provide an example of how these terms were used interchangeably in the first century.[11]

Note also that Peter does not refer to "the elder in each city," as though a single elder/pastor will suffice in each church. Apart from reference to one particular elder, as in the case of Peter, New Testament church elders are always in a plurality. No rule is given regarding the size of plurality, but there must be a plurality. Again, the great nineteenth-century Southern Baptist Convention leader, W. B. Johnson, provides some help:

> Whilst a plurality of bishops [elders] is required for each church, the number is not fixed, for the obvious reason, that circumstances must necessarily determine what the number shall be. In a church where more than one cannot be obtained, that one may be appointed upon the principle, that as soon as another can be procured there shall be a plurality.[12]

Such plurality helps to provide a greater measure of wisdom and leadership for the congregation. A larger mixture of spiritual gifts to serve the body will be present. These men are able to seek the Lord on critical issues facing the congregation in order to come to a sense of unity on the Lord's direction. They hold one another accountable as examples for the flock.

By Experience

Peter understood all of this firsthand because of his experience among the elders of Jerusalem.[13] But he also understood what these men were enduring in terms of the pressure facing them as Christians in the province of Asia Minor. So he identifies himself as their "fellow elder and witness of the sufferings of Christ, and a partaker also of the glory that is to be revealed." Since Peter, along with the other disciples (except John), fled our Lord during the time of His crucifixion, he is not referring to his "witness" as being the eyewitness account of what took place at Golgotha. Instead, the word *witness* literally means, "to testify of something." Peter was implying that he had joined these men in testifying of the sufferings of Christ, that is, all that He endured on behalf of us to redeem us from our sin. Peter witnessed the agony of Christ in Gethsemane, and what followed at Calvary. He understood Jesus Christ had redeemed them "with precious blood, as of a lamb unblemished and spotless, the blood of Christ" (1 Peter 1: 19). He was also an eyewitness to Christ's glory displayed in the Transfiguration and the Resurrection (1 Peter 1:3; 2 Peter 1:16–18). Maintaining the centrality of the gospel, Peter assures his fellow elders that they were *partners together in the work of the gospel.*

He also had an eye on the future. These brethren, along with Peter, would be sharing in (literally, fellowshipping in) the radiant glory of the revelation of Jesus Christ.[14] This was the hope that became an anchor for their souls in the midst of persecution.

HOW DO ELDERS AND THE CONGREGATION FUNCTION? (1 PETER 5:2–5)

Having identified himself with the elders in terms of position, passion for the gospel, and hope in Christ, Peter now asserts what is to be done within congregational life. How are elders to function? How is the congregation to respond?

Elders' Responsibility

"Shepherd the flock of God among you, exercising oversight," Peter wrote (v. 2). The verbs, *shepherd* and *exercising oversight* are the synonyms for "elder" in verb form.[15] These are the same terms (one as a noun, the other as a verb) used by Paul in Acts 20:28 when he spoke to the Ephesian elders: "Be on guard for yourselves and for all the flock, among which the Holy Spirit has made you overseers, to shepherd the church of God which He purchased with His own blood." Both of these terms encapsulate the elders' responsibility in the church.

As those who "shepherd the flock of God," elders are to give pastoral oversight to the congregation. A shepherd knows his sheep, watches out for dangers on their behalves, ensures that they are well fed and watered, applies healing balm to their wounds, and occasionally disciplines them to return them to the fold. Such a picture helps us to see how elders function. They watch over the souls of those under their charge (Heb. 13:17). They spend time with their flock, understanding their needs, and applying to them with precision the Word of God. They regularly feed them upon the truth of Scripture, unfolding the doctrines of the Word to help them stand firmly in the faith. John Calvin explained, "Let us bear in mind the definition given of the word [shepherd]; for the flock of Christ cannot be fed except with pure doctrine, which alone is our spiritual food."[16] Elders exercise wisdom in offering counsel through the Scriptures. As the shepherd led the way for the sheep, so the elders demonstrate their leadership, both in spiritual growth and Christian service. They are to set the example for Christian living, particularly as Peter explained in 1 Peter 2:11–3:16. J. H. Jowett wrote, "If a man stand between his brother and spiritual necessity, or between his brother and spiritual peril, he is discharging the office of a day's-man, a mediator, a faithful undershepherd, working loyally under the leadership of the 'chief Bishop and Shepherd of our souls.'"[17]

An elder is involved in "exercising oversight," which more formally describes shepherding, with perhaps more emphasis on the administrative and organizational elements of pastoral care. The early elders were admonished to labor in guarding the flock from false teachers. In the early church, transient spiritual rogues made their way into communities and threw congregations into disarray. Elders diligently labored to ensure that the church maintained solid doctrinal footing and that the members were equipped to resist the influence of false teachers. Today's elders do the same. When a member of the congregation falls prey to false teaching, the elders, as a shepherd would go after a wandering sheep, pursue that member. Such oversight is not merely a need of past centuries but a dire need for the present. Elders also organize the congregational care and ministry of teaching to assure the ongoing stability of the church. Well-fed and well-cared-for sheep have less reason to wander from the fold and into danger.[18]

Elders' Disposition

Along with the responsibility of spiritual leadership also comes much authority. Elders cannot lead or discipline unless they have some measure of authority. We tend to shy away from any use of the word *authority* in our day, perhaps fearing dictatorial maniacs. No one denies that such egotistical despots exist in church ranks, yet we must never abandon biblical direction because of a few poor examples. As long as a church insists upon the biblical pattern for its elders, seeking men with the disposition Peter describes, it need not fear its elders.

Motivation for service. Some people serve churches because others have talked them into it or because they have been manipulated by guilt until they accept the positions. But consider Peter's words: "exercising oversight not under compulsion but voluntarily, according to the will of God" (1 Peter 5:2), or literally, according to God. *Compulsion* refers to someone being forced or constrained to do something.[19] Perhaps, for example, a congregation asks a man to serve, but he declines because he does not believe he has the character to do the job or because he has no desire to serve. Instead of accepting the man's refusal, members keep approaching him, telling him that the church cannot survive without him, or threatening that they will leave the church if he does not take the position. If such a man takes the job, he would be serving according to man's will, not God's. All who serve the church must resist fleshly compulsion. Instead, they are to serve with a willing heart under a sense of divine direction, thus "according to the will of God."

What happens in terms of the quality and dedication of a person when he does so voluntarily rather than under constraint? He works harder because he desires to work. He finds joy in what he is doing. He possesses a sense of "staying power" that does not give up when times become difficult. He is able to deal more readily with discouragement.

The great motivation for serving as elders comes when men seek the Lord and become convinced that such service is the will of God for their lives. "Elders had to have courage and to be willing to accept this difficult task," writes Peter Jeffreys concerning the elders of the first century. "They had to want to place themselves in the front line of the battle against Satan. They had to be prepared for all the criticism which sometimes comes the way of church leaders." Moreover, "There were very severe troubles awaiting anyone who took on the office of an elder in those days."[20] Knowing that they are centered in the will of God gives elders a right perspective upon the office in light of its demands and pressures. Encouragement in the work comes, too, through the congregation's affirming God's will by its selection of the men to serve as *its* elders. The council of elders or presbytery affirms God's will by their thorough investigation of the elder candidates. The peace of the Lord fills the elders' hearts in regard to the sense of responsibility concerning the task before them. So now they can serve, facing the demands of the office with joy and thankfulness, knowing that they serve by the will of God.

Affection toward service. The motive to an elder's service must never be found in remuneration, but in a zeal for serving Christ. His service is to be "not for sordid gain, but with eagerness" (v. 2). At the time the passage was written, some among the body of elders evidently were being compensated for the time of their service. Paul makes reference to compensation in 1 Timothy 5:17–18: "The elders who rule well are to be considered worthy of double honor, especially those who work hard at preaching and teaching. For the Scripture says, 'YOU SHALL NOT MUZZLE THE OX WHILE HE IS THRESHING,' and 'The laborer is worthy of his wages.'" As the responsibilities of elders unfolded, some proved to be especially gifted in ministry areas that demanded more time than other ministries. Preaching and teaching, for instance, are not only more time consuming offices, they lead to church expansion. Thus, it seemed fitting for elders who preached and taught to be fairly remunerated. Not all elders are compensated, yet for those who receive compensation, money must never become the reason for service.

Elders must love what they do so that their service is "with eagerness," or full of zeal. *Eagerness* suggests strong enthusiasm for the duties of the office,[21] and might be translated "devoted zeal." Rather than the "sordid gain" of money or fame or power or attention, the elders serve with zealous devotion out of love for Christ and His church. Elders find their greatest satisfaction in acts of service, in what they give rather than in what they get.

Attitude in service. One of the grave dangers attending any sense of authority—whether in government, business, church, or even the home—is a haughty, dictatorial spirit. Peter exhorts, "Nor yet as lording it over those allotted to your charge, but proving to be examples to the flock." No one would dispute that powermongers occasionally creep into churches, desiring to exercise an iron grip on everything done in a congregation. They want to make all the decisions—whether regarding finances, sermon content, or church activities. I have heard shocking stories from pastors and church members who have faced such "little dictators." By intimidation, such persons sometimes manage to keep an entire congregation under their sway. That is not Christian leadership!

To discourage such despotic leadership, Peter reminds the elders that they serve at the pleasure of the Chief Shepherd. They are dealing with "the flock of God . . . allotted to your charge" (1 Peter 5:2–3). The terminology suggests the Master parceling out portions of His flock to this shepherd or that shepherd, with the understanding that *they will report to Him for the discharge of their duties.* Consequently, they are never to lord over the flock since the flock has one Lord, Jesus Christ.[22] Instead, they are to prove themselves "to be examples to the flock" (1 Peter 5:3). The word *example* means "a pattern." If a little girl makes paper dolls, she first finds a pattern, then traces around the pattern onto her paper to make the dolls. Or when a manufacturer produces an automobile, he utilizes a series of patterns, or dies, to produce the precise parts needed. Peter describes the elders as "Christians with skin on them" who demonstrate how to live the Christian life in all circumstances. That is a weighty responsibility, but much needed in the church.

Congregation's Response

How is the congregation to respond to the elders? "You younger men, likewise, be subject to your elders" (1 Peter 5:5). Bible students debate this text, with some suggesting that it points to simply the matter of age. Others explain "you younger men" as "not ordinary members of the church, but lower clergy, for example deacons, who are to serve like the elders (thus 'likewise') but also be subject to them."[23] But the context insists on a different direction. Typically, the elders of the congregation would have been those with more experience. Peter identifies particular members of the congregation as "younger men," who are to subject themselves to the leadership of the elders. Peter Davids comments, "It appears best, therefore, to see the 'younger' here as the youthful people in the church (if Jewish reckoning is involved, anyone under 30 and perhaps even some who were older would be included in this category)."[24] These "younger men" were living under the fire of persecution yet they had burning within them the passion to spread abroad the gospel. They would likely have the tendency to launch into risky actions, which could prove harmful to the whole church or detrimental to the work of the gospel. "Their very readiness for service and commitment," adds Davids, "can make them impatient with the leaders, who either due to pastoral wisdom or the conservatism that often comes with age (the two are not to be equated) are not ready to move as quickly or as radically as they are."[25] The younger men needed Peter's sage counsel of submitting themselves to the elders, and to continue walking with submissive hearts under the God-given authority of the elders. But that does not mean that elders were to act as killjoys.

Humility must clothe both elders and congregation: "And all of you, clothe yourselves with humility toward one another, for God is opposed to the proud, but gives grace to the humble" (1 Peter 5:5). This instruction is not just for the members of the congregation, but for the elders as well. The term *clothe* utilizes a Greek word that referred to a slave tying on an apron over his seamless garment while going about his work. The apron was a sign of the humble position of the slave.[26] So Peter reminds all the brethren that humility marks the church as genuine.

Being an elder does not mean that a man is better than others in the church, for "all of you clothe yourselves with humility toward one another." Nor can we assume that being an elder excludes a man from diligent Christian living, for elders must "prove to be examples to the flock" (1 Peter 5:3). Elders serve not out of constraint or earthly reward or even thought of grand recognition, but with a sense of God's call to this office so that they can serve with enthusiasm.

WHO HOLDS THE ELDERS ACCOUNTABLE? (1 PETER 5:4)

All of the exhortations become words to take seriously when we consider that both elders and congregation must one day stand before the Lord. As was observed in the previous chapter, each elder will face ultimate responsibility for his watching over the souls of those allotted to his charge, for elders serve "as those who will give an account" (Heb. 13:17). The congregation must recognize the God-given leadership found in the office of elder and submit to such leadership knowing that to fail in "this would be unprofitable for you" (v. 17). Both congregation and elders are accountable to the Chief Shepherd.

The Lord's Flock

The church does not belong to the elders, the pastor, or even the members of the congregation. The church belongs to Christ. That must burn in our hearts if we are to accept the biblical teaching for church order and life. Peter calls the church "the flock of God," as though it were a group of sheep that had been entrusted by the Chief Shepherd to a group of shepherds (elders) to oversee. "In using the imagery of tending God's flock," explains Paul Achtemeier, "the author is drawing on a long OT tradition, in which God is the shepherd of his people Israel, a tradition that may well have taken its origin in the tradition that God led his people out of bondage like a shepherd leads his sheep."[27] First Peter 5:3 reminds the elders that the church they serve has been "allotted to your charge."

Jesus Christ laid down his life for the sheep. Jesus Christ called them out of darkness and into the light of relationship to Himself. The sheep hear the voice of Jesus Christ, not the voice of a stranger; the sheep follow Jesus Christ, not mere men. Jesus Christ gives eternal life to the sheep so that none of them will perish. They are not held in the hands of mere elders, but held securely by the Father and the Son (John 10:1–30). So elders hold a stewardship before the Chief Shepherd for His sheep.

Service as an Undershepherd

All who serve as elders must remember that they are undershepherds, while Jesus Christ is the Chief Shepherd. One day the Chief Shepherd will appear and those belonging to Him will be gathered for eternity. Those whom He has appointed to serve as undershepherds will give an account for the way they have watched over the flock. The reward for service lies beyond this life. "The unfading crown of glory" is the Lord's gift for faithful service. "Lest, then, the faithful servant of Christ should be broken down," encourages Calvin, "there is for him one and only remedy,—to turn his eyes to the coming of Christ. Thus it will be, that he, who seems to derive no encouragement from men, will assiduously go on in his labours [sic], knowing that a great reward is prepared for him by the Lord."[28]

Scripture imparts the sense that *every* member of the congregation should serve humbly, voluntarily, and zealously, seeking to be examples to others in the body. But the qualities of service, humility, and zeal should be the particular hallmark of those men whom God raises up to serve as elders. The coin of responsibility has two sides: the congregation must acknowledge the men who serve as elders, and the elders must be faithful according to the instructions of God's Word.

REFLECTIONS

- How does the New Testament identify spiritual leaders in the church?
- In what ways do elders and the congregation function together in ministry?
- What should motivate the elders to serve?

PART THREE

From Theory to Practice

CHAPTER SEVEN

Thinking About Transition to Elder Leadership

What is involved in considering transition to plural eldership? No church or pastor should rush into an elder leadership structure. Careful thought, study, and planning must precede any changes, because implementing drastic changes too quickly might actually do the church more harm than good.

First, it is important to take a candid look at your church's polity. This entails a review of the church's constitution, bylaws, or other governing documents—including an assessment of how the church *actually* functions. Many church constitutions, for example, call for congregational rule, but a deacon board or group of trustees or a church staff may be the actual ruling authority. Assessing how your church operates and evaluating it in light of God's Word is the starting point.

On one end of the church polity spectrum lies pure congregationalism. The congregation decides on *everything,* resulting in endless discussions, haggling, posturing, and voting—and little accomplishment. Pure congregationalism thus holds little prospect for efficiency. Indeed, for those very reasons, few churches operate in a true congregational mode. Human relationships require leadership, and in a congregational setting, power often resides in a board of deacons. They usually receive at-large nomination and approval by the congregation, and serve either with or without tenure rotation. In many churches, though, such nominations are based on popularity or visibility within the church, without regard to the qualifications stated in 1 Timothy 3. Screening and examination find little place in the process. Moreover, the deacons—whose biblical role is one of service to the congregation—are put into the role of ruling the church. In such circumstances, power struggles often emerge between the pastor and the deacons. Rather than working together, they resort to political manipulation to accomplish agendas. Certainly not all deacons or pastors engage in such manipulative behavior, but my observations during three decades in ministry suggest such is a frequent scenario.

On the other end of the polity spectrum are churches in which the senior pastor has his thumb on everything in the church. He might be what W. A. Criswell termed "a benevolent dictator," who considers his leadership more efficient than a plural eldership that must work toward consensus on church issues. He simply makes the declaration and all are obliged to follow. Or he might be a ruthless tyrant, a controlling pastor, like Diotrephes, who covets preeminence in the local church so that he excludes anyone who threatens his position (3 John 9–10). His unteachable spirit makes him unapproachable and insensitive to pastoral needs. The church seems to exist to further his agenda and feed his ego.

Megachurches face the greatest danger at this point because of the enormous pressure on them to exceed past performance, as measured by the previous year's statistics.

Another type of polity, one much less tyrannical, can be found in some pastor-staff led churches. In these churches, the pastor and staff determine the course of ministry, tap the lay leadership to service their plans, and harness the energies of the church into a well-oiled machine. Some even identify this as their plurality of elders. Certainly, many of these churches accomplish much—as long as there are no changes in the machinery. The machinery may grind to a halt, however, if change does occur (e.g., a staff vacancy). When conflicts arise between pastor and staff, such are often concealed in order to preserve the appearance of harmony. Highly organized activity may cover a reality of unholiness in life and conduct. Megachurches face the greatest danger at this point because of the enormous pressure on them to exceed past performance, as measured by the previous year's statistics. Unhealthy competition with other churches can drive them to mask conflicts that reveal a lack of true spirituality within the leadership.

Variations of these models can be found, but common to each is the problem of those in leadership competing with each other for power and authority. There is a better way—elder leadership. Making the transition to elder leadership within a congregational framework requires deliberate work, faithful praying, and commitment to the teaching of Scripture. In 1987, when John Piper led the Bethlehem Baptist Church of Minneapolis to change its church polity, he offered a number of reasons for reexamining their governance and transitioning to elder plurality. He called attention to the need for "conforming to the normal New Testament pattern," and for clarifying the role of their deacons. (He described that role as "a hybrid" that existed as a governing board while retaining the name of deacons.) He also called for the "need to provide more thorough care for hurting members and more consistent discipline for delinquent members," suggesting that the confusion in leadership roles might be the cause for neglect. Piper ended with a challenge to go beyond staff leadership in developing well-grounded roots of lay leadership in the church. "We need to develop an ongoing leadership team (elders) where the theological distinctives, the philosophy of ministry and the vision of the future can be rooted more durably than in the paid 'staff.' The church should not be dependent on a few paid staff as the guardians of the vision."[1]

With elder leadership, multi-staff led (ruled) churches face a new level of accountability beyond that of simply exceeding statistical performance. When plural eldership takes root, statistical benchmarks will be replaced by the benchmarks of character and Christian walk, faithfulness in obedience, commitment to genuine church unity, diligence in improving family life, and zeal for equipping the church for ministry. Some program-driven staff members might not fit into elder leadership. Thus, if this office is to function properly, elder qualifications must not be presumed even for staff members.

I have talked with many pastors who long to have elders join them in equal authority rather than the pastors seeming to hold church authority in their own grip. Seeing fellow pastors fall into disgrace through moral or financial failures has strengthened the desire of many to transition into plural eldership for the sake of accountability. Some pastors, however, tightly grip the reins of authority in their churches, often shunning accountability by exaggerating their own strength and ability. By refusing to share authority, they create a dangerous climate for failure. As a pastor, Jeff Noblit first considered elder leadership because he feared the temptations of power. Noblit became senior pastor of the First Baptist Church of Muscle Shoals, Alabama—the largest Southern Baptist congregation in the northwest corner of the state—after serving for almost a decade as student minister and associate pastor in the same church. Muscle Shoals is a city of less than 15,000, although the region's population exceeds 100,000. Noblit's predecessor, the church's first pastor, functioned as a "single elder." The former pastor was well liked in both the church and the community, and had been quite successful in his ministry. Moreover, he was *the* authority in the church, with the church's deacons functioning ably in a service role. Although the church occasionally voted on major issues, such voting was usually a formality with the pastor's desires ratified.

Shortly after Noblit assumed the role of senior pastor, he faced a major disciplinary crisis in the church that involved removing high profile members from the membership. Although church discipline had not been practiced in the past, Pastor Noblit guided the church through the initial process and gained the respect and admiration of the congregation. But the downside came, according to Noblit, when he realized that he had too much authority vested in him as pastor. He told me that he was afraid of such unrestricted power and that he desired accountability. That formed the basis for moving in the direction of elder leadership. Noblit's experience is described in greater detail later in this chapter.

One of the largest hurdles on the path to plural eldership involves "governing deacons" (i.e., deacons who rule the business of the church). In settings where such men lack biblical qualifications for office, giving up that esteemed position for newly formed plural eldership comes hard. In some settings, deacons only need to be taught the Scriptures and they will gladly conform to the biblical model. In others it might take years for the pastor to cultivate change through biblical exposition that regularly applies the Bible to real life. However well intentioned, a blunt announcement of a change from deacon leadership to elder leadership—absent the necessary biblical teaching, and demonstration of commitment to the congregation—will likely lead to resistance by the deacons. Deacons can help facilitate the change to elder leadership—as one pastor discovered.

"Having elders was the most important change that has happened here in support of my own ministry and goals for the church," commented Mark Dever, Senior Pastor of the Capitol Hill Baptist Church in Washington, D.C. Dever faced an uphill challenge with the declining membership in this urban congregation, just four blocks from the nation's Capitol. He initiated a two-year process of revising the church's constitution and bylaws, helped by Matt Schmucker, who at that time served as church administrator. Dever and Schmucker completed the initial revision, calling for elder leadership in a congregational setting, and then passed the recommendations to the church's deacon board. The deacon board made further revisions and then passed the work to an *ad hoc* committee of deacons and non-deacons formed for a year. This group then formed a larger group of thirty deacons and non-deacons to dialogue on changes before presenting the revision to the church at large. Two or three membership meetings were called for the express purpose of reviewing the proposed changes to the constitution. The congregation voted almost unanimously for the changes, including installation of elders, with only one nay vote. This church's transition is described more fully later in the chapter.

A pastor desiring plural eldership is wise not to introduce this change until he has established trust with the congregation. This may take several years of faithfully ministering to the congregation so that the pastor no longer appears to be an outsider. As the congregation grows to trust other biblically-based pastoral decisions, a greater possibility exists for transition to biblical eldership under the pastor's leadership. Establishing a basis of mutual trust no doubt runs at the heart of transitioning from any type of polity to elder plurality. Trust comes through longevity, faithfulness in pastoral responsibilities, genuine humility, and deep reverence for applying the gospel to all of life. I try to discourage pastors from leading their churches to elder plurality if they have no intention of staying with their flocks. Pastoral "ladder climbers" lack the depth and stamina necessary to help a congregation through the transition.

WE'VE NEVER DONE IT THIS WAY BEFORE!

- Plural eldership unites staff and non-staff members in leadership equality.
- Plural eldership refocuses the spotlight in church life.
- Plural eldership provides a new level of efficiency.

"We've never done it this way before!" are the so-called seven last words of the church. Elder plurality is unlike other methods of church leadership—benevolent dictatorships, deacon rule, and staff rule. *Elder plurality unites paid staff with non-staff members of the congregation*, governing and teaching the church in equality. Elder plurality assures the congregation that multiple eyes, ears, and hearts are turned toward members' needs and are committed to leading them spiritually. While this can happen in other structural models, when the biblical model is followed, pastoral ministry increases, and overall church life conforms in greater degree to genuine Christianity. So even though "we've never done it this way before," we must ask ourselves why we have not, and examine what biblical foundation (if any) we have for our existing church structure. Such risky questions set the stage either for transitioning to elder plurality or exposing unwillingness to submit to the teaching of Scripture.

Plural eldership refocuses the spotlight in church life. Often the church staff or pastor or deacon chairman receives undue attention by the congregation. That approach to church leadership has long crippled churches. But the goal of elder plurality dismantles crippling power structures, redirecting attention to the glory of Christ. Plurality thus humbles the natural pride involved in leadership, and gives a constant reminder that the church exists for the glory of Christ, not the aggrandizement of one man, or a few men.

In the process of sharing authority, individuals involved in leadership may from time to time not get their way in some aspect of church life or ministry. Even in elder plurality, the fallibility of the men united in shepherding the church can surface in poor decisions, power struggles, and self-centered desires. Elders must never presume upon their spiritual lives but must seek to discipline themselves for the purpose of godliness (1 Tim. 4:6–10). Through prayer, discussion, studying the Scriptures, and the illuminating wisdom of godly men laboring together, clearer direction will be forged in church decisions. As a result, the health and effectiveness of the church takes precedence over the plans of one person.

Elder plurality provides a new level of efficiency in church life. While a pastor or church staff may make decisions more quickly, they may tend to do so without sensitivity to the overall congregation. Non-staff elders see some things that those involved in full-time Christian ministry cannot. Those of us in vocational ministry find this difficult to admit. The constant saturation of experience within the walls of ministry, however, may skew a pastor's thinking on congregational expectations and needs. I have learned to lean heavily upon the wisdom of our non-staff elders, recognizing that they have unique insight in evaluating issues. During a particularly difficult time financially, our non-staff elders recommended a course of informing and challenging the congregation to rise to a new level in giving. Frankly, I was at a loss on how to best proceed but these men wisely detailed a plan—without any sort of manipulation or cunning—that helped the church membership to understand the critical need and how God might be pleased to meet that need. The plan succeeded, thanks to the elders' sensitivity to both the financial needs and the congregation's ability under God to meet it.

Such insights often occur during the trying times in ministry. I had been involved in counseling a couple having marital problems. The problems were distressing, although workable, but I seemed unable to bridge the gap that glared between the husband and wife. One of our non-staff elders joined me in visiting the couple. We both spoke clearly and passionately about marriage and the need for reconciliation. After we left I still felt puzzled on how to deal with them. Their situation weighed heavily on me as though I felt singularly responsible to put their marriage back together. I asked the elder, "What did you think?" He wisely discerned, "There's something they're not telling that lies beneath the problems. Until they come clean, your counseling will prove futile. You've done what you can. Now we have no choice but to pursue a course of discipline." I realized that this couple's marital problems were not my burden alone, but one that was shared by my fellow elders, and was supported by their insightful understanding of marriage and integrity.

Establishing elder plurality requires changing existing governing documents to reflect the new polity. A church must never simply begin plural eldership, ignoring its constitution, bylaws, and policies. By doing so, recourse could be taken later to disrupt the entire structure. Sharp minds, steeped in the Scripture and biblical theology, must lead the way in reordering governing documents.

Congregational approval of the changes is, of course, also necessary. Elder plurality should never be foisted on a church. Instead, by undertaking to instruct the congregation, engaging their comments and questions, a pastor can facilitate a smooth transition in governance.

CHURCH PROFILES

- Does it really work?
- How can a church transition to elder plurality?

Two questions might come to mind while evaluating this study on plural eldership. First, does it really work in church life? Because of the undue influence of pragmatism in our day, many neglect stepping out in dependence on the veracity of God's Word. While mere pragmatic concerns must never drive our practice, plural eldership does, indeed, work well in congregational life when churches take seriously the pattern of Scripture.[2] The second question does have practical implications: How can we transition to elder plurality? This question will be addressed in another chapter. But the stories of some churches that have walked through the transition to plural eldership will help put a face to these questions. These churches have not only lived to tell about the transition, but have found elder leadership to be better than expected.

From Pastor's Council to Elders

Jeff Noblit, a committed expositor, began the transition to biblical eldership by preaching for eight weeks through 1 Timothy 3 and Titus 1 on the qualifications and roles of elders. He placed special emphasis on the qualifications without being immediately concerned with the specific title to be adopted. Afterward, he led the church to vote on nominating men to serve as a "Pastor's Council." Thinking that the use of the title *Elder* might overwhelm the Baptist congregation, Noblit chose *Pastor's Council* as a substitute. Nevertheless, the qualifications and roles for the Pastor's Council were clearly that of the New Testament elder. Among other responsibilities, the duties of the Pastor's Council included planning for personnel, finance, and long-range goals. After a slate of men were nominated, Noblit screened the nominees, and presented a pared down list to the church body for affirmation.

When asked how the church responded to this new change in leadership, Noblit commented that the congregation offered strong support, and particularly appreciated the accountability now established for the pastor and other leaders in the church. The Pastor's Council expected Pastor Noblit to lead, and counted him as "first among equals" in their Council. Over a period of time the name *Pastor's Council* was dropped and the title of *Elders* adopted for this leadership group. Noblit commented that the elder leadership in his church has been "wonderfully effective." He said that they continue to "really strive to make sure that they [the elders] are biblically qualified," and if an elder fails to maintain the type of character and practice needed among elders, he is asked to step down from service.[3]

Teaching, Teaching, Teaching

In a conversation, Matt Schmucker emphasized that the lengthy, two-year process of changing polity structure to reflect plural eldership was essential for Capitol Hill Baptist Church in Washington, D.C. It demonstrated to the church that no one was rushing through unbiblical or thoughtless changes. Senior Pastor Mark Dever and the leaders deliberately worked to expand circles of discussion so that the whole congregation might embrace the changes enthusiastically. Schmucker commented that central to the process was "teaching, teaching, teaching," capped by an insightful congregational talk by New Testament scholar, Don Carson. Carson pointed out the normalcy of elders in the New Testament church, and booklets on elder leadership by John MacArthur and John Piper proved helpful in educating the congregation as well.

Initially, some reacted against the idea of elders out of fear of "ruling elders" in congregational structure. The slow process—and the maintaining of congregationalism with elder leadership—helped to bring about strong unanimity for the changes. The deacon board established a transition plan that called for Pastor Dever to nominate the first group of elders to serve the church. Schmucker admitted that some problems arose at this point, chiefly from some who were not nominated for the office. After working through that process, the church approved the first group of elders, and continues elder leadership today through rotating service. Capitol Hill Baptist Church's membership includes many men and women in their twenties and thirties who work in various agencies related to the government. Thus, identifying and developing qualified elders from among the young and educated members of the congregation is an ongoing agenda for the church. Schmucker stressed that the elders labor to teach the congregation and shape young men for the high responsibilities of the eldership. In addition to teaching the church, their elders, he said, primarily engage in prayer for the membership as well as prayer accountability for each other. The elders maintain responsibility for the church's membership classes and shepherding the congregation.[4]

My Own Story

Developing church polity from the ground up is part of church planting. In 1987, I began work as the founding pastor of South Woods Baptist Church in Memphis, Tennessee, with the church constituting in January 1988. Since South Woods—a suburban church—had no congregational history or traditions to protect, establishing polity worked differently than in the other churches just described. Initial leadership definitely rested on my shoulders, but I soon formed a "steering committee" to help guide this new flock through the sometimes murky waters of developing a viable church. The steering committee helped with decision-making, and provided both short-term and long-range planning. Soon we realized that our loosely structured polity might lead to problems in the future, so we formed a "Pastor's Council." The Pastor's Council consisted of seven men who seemed to understand the spiritual state of health within the congregation. This council was an interim step in producing a permanent church structure. The council and I began a lengthy study of the biblical texts addressing church leadership, structure, decision-making, and any passages that might shape church polity. We decided that we would approach church structure with as little bias as possible so that we might better grapple with the biblical direction for the church. All of us were long-time Southern Baptists, so we were all familiar with issues of pastoral authority, deacon leadership, congregationalism, and the diverse ways in which these worked out in autonomous congregations. Each man understood some of the problems common to the structure of Baptist churches, problems that we desired to avoid if possible. Our journey through the Scripture continued for about a year-and-a-half, and we kept copious notes on the study, and drew conclusions together. That laid the groundwork for elder leadership.

We knew that we must do more than simply inform the congregation of the proposed structure—the people had to be taught as well. I began a three-month series of expositions on Sunday evenings that addressed each of the biblical texts that our Pastor's Council had studied. I sought not only to explain the texts, but also to make application to our own situation. The studies were often interspersed with question and answer sessions. These sessions helped our members work through the difficulties of confronting tradition with biblical truth. After completing this study with the congregation, we voted unanimously to adopt elder leadership for our church. Although the vote was unanimous, during the process a couple of families left because of disagreement over elder leadership. Lastly, the change was codified in a new "Policy and Procedure Manual," which served as our bylaws.

Like Mark Dever, I found the establishment of plural eldership to be the most important step in strengthening my ministry and ensuring stability in our church. Not every step has gone smoothly. The initial group of elders, for the most part, lacked the maturity needed to walk through the demands upon pastoral leaders. Still, the congregation's respect for the eldership was instrumental in the group's enhancing the church's ministry. As the congregation matured, the Lord raised up other men to replace the initial group so that today we have an outstanding body of elders leading our church. I am privileged to work side-by-side with these men in directing the ministry of our church and in training the body for ministry. We pray together, teach together, share together our joys and burdens, and hold one another accountable as Christian leaders. The blending of different personalities, gifts, strengths, and even weaknesses continues to hone us as spiritual leaders. The trust developed between our eldership and the congregation has become a precious treasure to guard. I often remind our elders that nothing can do greater harm to our church than for this trust to be broken by carelessness in our spiritual lives or duties.

REFLECTIONS

- Describe your own church's polity.
- In what ways does your church conform to *or* conflict with plural eldership?
- How can plural eldership change the dynamics in a local church?
- What are some key considerations in transitioning to plural eldership?

CHAPTER EIGHT

Can It Be Done?

Making the Transition to Elder Leadership

A pastor of a large Southern Baptist church recently contacted me. He wanted to discuss transitioning from congregational rule to an elder-led church polity. "I need to decide," he said, "if this is a hill worth dying on." He understood that in the traditional Southern Baptist setting there might be a concerted reaction in transitioning to an elder-led church. He's not standing alone. Many pastors and church leaders contemplate the same concern as they begin to understand the biblical teaching of church leadership. Some rush into the process without laying the proper groundwork and end up with major church conflict that often culminates in the pastor being dismissed from leadership. How, then, does one begin the transition?

Begin slowly. This is not a process to be completed overnight. Forms of leadership, patterns on decision making, and engrained habits of church life rarely change quickly. So if one begins this process, it needs to be seen through to the end.

Brief pastorates fail to build the trust necessary to shift from one form of church government to one grounded on God's Word. A pastor's being faithful in the teaching of the Scripture concerning the nature of the church, the believer's relationship to the church, the authority and responsibilities of leaders, the unity of the body, and other doctrines related to a

New Testament church—all this takes time to be realized in the collective mind of a congregation. Foundational to teaching on ecclesiology are the doctrines related to the inspiration of Scripture, the doctrine of God, the person and work of Christ, soteriology, and the person and work of the Holy Spirit. Faithful exposition of God's Word will give the pastor the opportunity to deal with each of these doctrines as he works his way year-by-year through books of the Bible. *Only when a church begins to think biblically will elder-led leadership seem plausible.*

The following process is recommended for establishing elder-led leadership in congregations. This approach can be varied for adaptation to individual settings, but note that completion of the process will likely take at least eighteen months to three years—perhaps longer. It may be helpful to divide the process into three phases.

Evaluation Phase	Presentation Phase	Implementation Phase
• Assess	• Exposition	• Pray
• Study	• Discussion	• Screen
• Probe	• Qualifications	• Ordain Elders
• Summarize		• Involve
		• Review

EVALUATION PHASE

Assess

Who are the leaders in your congregation? They are given different titles, for example, deacons, stewards, trustees, board members, church council, teachers, small-group leaders, committee chairmen, staff members. Take the time to evaluate how each leader functions. What kinds of standards are already in place for these leadership roles? How many truly demonstrate godly leadership? Who appears to enjoy the title and recognition but does not exhibit dependable servant leadership? Who is teachable? Who demonstrates the heart to pay the price of servant leadership?

Who has the ear of the congregation? Ask the tough and probing questions, and make necessary reflection and evaluation.

The pastor will constantly need to seek the Lord throughout the transition process, but especially during the initial stages when he lays groundwork for elders. He will need to size up the current leaders' understanding of basic doctrine, grasp of spiritual authority, commitment to servant leadership, and determination to obey the Lord of the church at all costs. The pastor will need to direct his teaching, preaching, and training to fill the gaps in these areas. To accomplish this, it will be necessary to teach some leaders in a one-on-one or small-group setting. Other leaders will respond well to the pastor's pulpit expositions. It should be recognized that some leaders will, of course, balk at any change in leadership structure. The pastor must labor to be gentle with those in opposition and yet stand faithfully upon the truth of God's Word.

It is recommended that the pastor narrow the leadership core of the church to a manageable group and invite them to join the pastor for a thorough study of every biblical passage addressing leadership, decision making, church structure, and all that falls under the realm of church polity. At such a time the pastor will need to lead the group in properly interpreting each text in its historical, linguistic, and theological context. The pastor might need to begin with basic principles of hermeneutics. It is not recommended at the onset to use study guides or books on elders. That should come later. Rather, open the Word of God and allow the leadership core to see what Scripture sets forth for the church. Basic exegetical tools, Bible dictionaries, concordances, and commentaries can be helpful during this round table dialogue. Ask questions of the texts. Maintain copious notes for later use. With an openness to obey the Word of God, face the passages that stand in clear opposition to the church's current polity. Give assignments to those involved so that they are *forced* to dig into the Word on their own in order to report their discoveries at the next meeting. Be open with each other, avoiding defensive posturing. Keep in mind the goal: leading the church to be biblical.

The pastor may become quite vulnerable during this study since he is leading the church to consider major changes in structure. If the church leaders are more concerned about holding their positions than obeying the revelation of Scripture, the pastor may be in for rocky times. Still, he must take the high road, emphasizing his desire to obey the Lord and to lead the church to obedience. The pastor must be patient yet firm, realizing that a heavy-handed insistence on his interpretation may prove counterproductive. During this time, the pastor and others who lead the study must model the godly leadership described throughout the New Testament. Expect the Lord to turn hearts, but give Him time to do so.

Study

First look at some of the Old Testament passages that in general fashion deal with leadership. There are plenty of examples, pro and con, but keep in mind that national structures do not equate to church structures. Ample models of godly leadership and its effects upon God's people will be evident, although it will unnaturally force the biblical text to create a New Testament church model from Old Testament national structures. Comparing and contrasting King Saul and King David's leadership can be helpful. Looking at the leadership principles in Joshua, Ezra, and Nehemiah might also help the study group to grapple with qualities necessary to lead a congregation. None of these examples, however, will adequately explain the New Testament church polity.[1]

Template for Studying Selected Texts from Acts
- Problem
- Solution
- Process

Move to the New Testament, studying every passage—in its context—related to leaders, leadership practices, leadership requirements, church structure, decision making, crises requiring decision in church life, and church conflicts. Many scholars discourage using the book of Acts as the basis for doctrine, but the best examples of church decision making and leadership will be found there. Acts, in fact, offers illustrations of what the epistles state in principle. At minimum, the study group will need to consider Acts 1:12–26; 6:1–7; 11:1–18; 11:19–26; 13:1–3; 14:21–23; 15:1–

41; 20:17–38; and 21:17–26. For consistency of interpretation, various passages should be analyzed in a threefold manner: *problem, solution, process.* Applying this analysis helps especially to understand how the early brethren arrived at decisions that affected church life and how leaders functioned in relationship to congregational life. The study group should also consider other texts, such as Matthew 18:15–20; 1 Corinthians 5:1–13; Ephesians 4:11–16; 1 Timothy 3:1–16; Titus 1:5–9; Hebrews 13:7, 17–19; and 1 Peter 5:1–5.

Pay close attention to the historical and cultural backgrounds in each text. Some of the passages might deal with specific problems that required an unrepeatable process to resolve. Make the distinction in your study, but learn from the principles unfolded. Notice the trends established that give evidence of ongoing practice for all churches. Do thorough work on word studies, grasping the use of words common in the first century that may have different implications today. Keep detailed notes of the discussions during each meeting, making them available to study-group members. Because of the nature of this kind of study, and to guard against the formation of improper conclusions, group members should limit their discussion of the study with the congregation at large. Until the leaders are able to share their conclusions with the congregation, it may suffice to notify the congregation that church leaders are doing a thorough study of the Scripture regarding church polity.

Probe

The more your leadership group can be involved in the intensive study, the better chance they will embrace the biblical pattern for church polity. Leaders need to know that they are part of something vital to the future of their church. For this reason, it is important that the pastor not do all the study and then just dump information into the group members' laps. Rather, give assignments and set expectations for study within the group. Help them understand how to use exegetical tools in their study; point them to commentaries, theological works, and word studies that might help them grapple with their assigned text. In the process, you will be discipling them. I worked through this same process with a leadership group. Although at the beginning some were opposed to elders in Baptist life, as they worked through the Scripture on their own, they arrived at a different conclusion. Seeing for themselves what the Scripture taught gave them a sense of ownership and determination to see the process through.

That having been said, the pastor must always do his homework first. There is no guarantee that someone assigned a text will know how to study and interpret it. So the pastor must be prepared to ask questions, make observations, and gently guide the group to the clear sense of the biblical texts. A good way to do this is to prepare probing questions for each text, such as the following:

- Why was there conflict in the early Jerusalem church as recorded in Acts 6:1–7?
- What kind of guidance did the apostles give to the church?
- What was the church's responsibility in addressing the conflict?
- How are the priorities of each type of church leader distinguished in the text?
- What were the issues that caused the early church's structure to emerge?
- Are the same kinds of needs present in our own church setting?
- How well does our church conform to this early church model?

Throughout the study the pastor will need to reinforce the importance of understanding and obeying the Word of God. We often make much of the Bible's inerrancy, but do we strive to believe and obey the inerrant Word? Are we willing to follow the Word of God regardless of what tradition or popular trends may demand? As can be seen, the critical issue in the whole process is our submission to the revelation of God through His Word.

Summarize

My own process of carrying a leadership group through a study of Scripture took a year and a half. We did not necessarily meet each week. But we did persist. All the while we recorded our findings and ultimately developed a brief summary for the congregation's perusal.

It is not suggested that the congregation be handed a long document regarding your study since most people will not take the time to read it. Try to narrow your thoughts into a one- or two-page summary, and perhaps prepare a lengthier document for those desiring to study the findings in detail. Stand together as a leadership group on what you have done. Give ample scriptural citations so that those interested might be able to investigate God's Word on their own. Above all, bring the force of your argument on church polity back to the one place of authority—the Word of God.

Your short summary will serve as a primer to stimulate questions and develop guidance for more detailed study. It will also become a proving ground for the church's commitment to Scripture. The next step will be critical in helping the congregation grapple with the teaching of God's Word.

PRESENTATION PHASE

Exposition

Biblical exposition is always the best way to approach change. Rather than stringing a group of verses together to prove one's point, the faithful expositor will open a text of Scripture and unfold it so that the congregation can understand the passage's message in its context. It will be helpful to preach through the texts that the leadership group wrestled through. I did this over a three-month period on Sunday evenings, and afterward often opened the floor for dialogue. I announced ahead of time that our leadership had worked through these texts, and that I now wanted to set forth our understanding of them for the whole church. The leadership team was also available to answer questions.

One or two weeks will not lay groundwork for transition, so take whatever time is needed to deal thoroughly with each text. Realize that in many settings church members have never heard the word "polity," and think that "elders" belong only to Presbyterians. Since Scripture interprets Scripture, the pastor will need to show the connection in the series of texts he lays before the church.

Some pastors may find that covering a short series in Acts, followed by an interlude of covering a different series before returning to another series in the Epistles, will allow the congregation time to absorb more fully the biblical teaching. Studies of 1 Timothy 3 and Titus 1, addressing qualifications, show those elders as representations of the gospel in the community. Exposition provides the best means for unfolding the contexts surrounding the passages and helping the congregation to understand how the early church's structure developed in the crucible of life.

Discussion

The leadership group's summary document may help to facilitate discussion after the sermon series (each pastor will have to determine what is best in his setting). It is not advisable to proceed to the discussion phase if the sermon series was not well attended and received. In that case, the church might not be ready, and forcing a discussion might result in needless conflict. Assuming all has gone well, ask the congregation to read the summary document and the biblical texts. Invite members to bring their questions into a congregational forum.

Bring the church body together for a time of discussing the leadership group's conclusions, as well as the content of the sermons. Openness and honesty about the differences between what the Word clearly teaches and what the church practices will help to bridge the understanding gap. Always go back to the Scripture as authority for changes, being careful not to make personal attacks on former leaders. Answer as many questions as possible, holding multiple dialogue sessions, if needed.

After the pastor and study-group members have answered the congregation's questions, ask the church to adopt the biblical structure for the church's own polity. Making such a decision could involve amending or removing the church's current constitution, or bylaws, or policy manual, or other governing documents. Some people, especially older members, consider church constitutions to be sacred property, so tampering with them may stir ire. You are blessed if you have older members in leadership who can speak appreciatively of the past, while supporting obedience for the future. The pastor and leadership need to show humility and patience in creating change, realizing that some still might not follow.

The pastor and leadership study group will need to develop the church's new governing document based on the group's understanding of Scrip-

ture. This new document will need the congregation's approval. At no
time should the congregation receive the impression that this document
is being crammed down their throats. Give members time to digest what
the new document means and how it will change church life. Granted,
some details of governance may be vague or unknown. But candor about
the existence of uncertainties will give the congregation confidence that
the burning desire of the leadership is to follow the Word of God and to
trust the Lord of the church to bless what He has entrusted to the churches.

Qualifications

Nothing is more critical in the elder-led structure than setting forth
biblical qualifications for church leaders. If the congregation understands
the requirements for being an elder, members will have greater respect
for the elder body. It is ironic that in their rush to transition to biblical
elder leadership, some churches underemphasize or overlook the biblical qualifications for individual elders. If the church transitions to elder
leadership but then installs as elders men who lack biblical qualifications, even greater problems may result. So be diligent at this point to
instruct the church properly.

Setting forth the biblical qualifications (e.g., 1 Tim. 3; Titus 1; 1 Peter
5) can be done through pulpit expositions (Sunday morning is preferable at this point because of the likelihood of more members being
present) or through Sunday school lessons on the subject. Printed material may also be helpful. The aim is for the entire church to know what is
expected in elders (and deacons as well). Knowledge about expectations
not only builds accountability for the elders to the congregation, it also
may deter wrongly motivated or otherwise disqualified men from pursuing eldership.

Some men who do not meet the biblical qualifications for eldership
may have been considered church leaders. Unless pride has been checked
in their lives, such men may revolt against the intense biblical standards.
Take their complaints back to the Word of God as the final arbiter of
church disputes. The church's mettle will be tested at just this point.

Setting an arbitrary number of elders for any church is inadvisable
because much depends on the spiritual maturity of the congregation.

Some churches begin by establishing a ratio system—one elder per a given number of members. Whatever number or ratio is established, quality must be emphasized over quantity. It is better to begin with a smaller group of well-qualified elders than to fill a quota with unqualified men. After the church has matured, the elders might recommend setting a certain number of elders, limiting their term of service, and establishing a rotation system to increase involvement. Above all, hold forth the biblical standards for church leaders.

IMPLEMENTATION PHASE

Pray

Before selecting elders, call the church body to prayer. Selecting a group of men to serve the church as spiritual leaders is a major step that will impact the total church life. Church members must understand the seriousness of such a decision and their own part in it, and collectively seeking the Lord's guidance will reinforce such seriousness. The church must also be aware that the adversary will attempt to scuttle plans to follow the teaching of Scripture. Be vigilant, then, in calling upon the Lord of the church to direct each step and decision.

Selecting qualified men to serve as elders is so important that the process should never be rushed. If the pastor and leadership group determine that the church currently has no men qualified for eldership, then teaching, developing, training, and praying must continue until the church can pursue elder leadership.

Screen

In narrowing the field of elder candidates, each church must establish a plan that works best for it. In some cases the senior pastor chooses the initial group of elder candidates and then takes them through the screening process, much the same way that Paul and Barnabas appointed elders during their first missionary journey (Acts 14:23). Once the elder body is established, these elders will nominate subsequent elders.[2] Mark Dever utilizes a quadrant to help evaluate candidates for elders.

(1) Central Christian Concerns	(2) Distinctive Theological Concerns
(4) Love for the Congregation	(3) Distinctive Cultural Concerns

When evaluating men who have the character and ability to serve as elders, the first matter should be (1) *Central Christian Concerns,* for example, faithful testimony as a Christian, ability to articulate the gospel, stable walk with Christ, consistent Christian character, and strong family life. The notable characteristics listed in 1 Timothy 3 and Titus 1 apply. If the man demonstrates faithfulness in this area, then (2) *Distinctive Theological Concerns* must be considered (Acts 20:28–31). This aims particularly at the candidate's position toward the church's doctrinal statement as well as his grasp of the faith. Such might be evidenced by his ability to articulate biblically the church's position on baptism or worship or evangelism or church government. Having shown understanding and ability to dialogue theologically, the next quadrant evaluates the (3) *Distinctive Cultural Concerns* that are presently affecting the church or Christian community, the role of women in the church, for example, or issues of modernity affecting the church, and effects of the church-growth movement on the church (Titus 1:9). The final quadrant assures that the elder candidate has applied his understanding of the gospel and theological issues to life in regard to (4) *Love for the Congregation* (1 Peter 5:2–3). Is there evidence that he genuinely loves the body of Christ and desires to serve and minister to the church?[3]

In other churches, members of the congregation nominate the initial group of elders for consideration and screening. The senior pastor, being an elder, must take the leadership at this point. He can feel free to ask two or three other godly men to assist him in this process, or even utilize elders from another church to hold him accountable during the process. Since our church was accustomed to congregationalism, I utilized membership in the elder candidating process. After preaching on the biblical qualifications for elders, I asked the congregation to nominate men whom they believed were biblically qualified to serve as elders. I provided a simple form that asked if the nominator had read and agreed to the biblical standards for elders in 1 Timothy 3 and Titus 1, and if the nominator believed that the nominee qualified on this basis. Then the nominator was asked to write a brief explanation of why he or she nominated a particular man to the office of elder (we do the same for deacon). This explanation sheds light on whether the nomination is based on the popularity of the nominee or on his servant-heartedness.

After allowing two weeks for nominations, the pastor—and any chosen beforehand to assist—will narrow the field of nominees. Some will be excluded due to circumstances in the nominee's life known to the pastor or others involved. Family concerns or personal habits or problems in other areas may disqualify the nominee. Disqualified nominees will be removed from consideration without making their nominations public.

The congregation needs to understand the sensitivity involved in screening candidates, and the need for complete confidentiality. Once the initial list is narrowed, the pastor will contact each nominee personally to ascertain his willingness to undergo the elder screening process and to serve if approved. Holding forth biblical standards seems to significantly narrow the field of nominations. Even some of those who initially accept nomination subsequently withdraw themselves after considering the seriousness of the office. My own church's practice at this point is to keep the names of the nominees private so that there is no embarrassment if a nominee is disqualified.

Those agreeing to nomination are then asked to complete a thorough doctrinal questionnaire. The nominee will write about his conversion and personal walk with Christ, explaining, too, his views on the gospel, the church, and the role of elders. He will need to study the church's doctrinal statement and completely affirm it or identify any areas of disagreement. The nominee will need as well to evaluate himself in light of the biblical qualifications for elders, addressing his family life, and his relationship to his wife and children. He will also explain why, if selected, he should serve as an elder and how he will seek to lead the congregation.

The written questionnaire must be taken seriously, for it asks the nominee to put in writing what he believes. It will also reveal whether or not he as a church leader can articulate the Christian faith and basic ecclesiology. Such a questionnaire might raise concerns about the nominee that need to be investigated. Or it might be the means of disqualifying him for service due to frank admissions about his walk with Christ or lack of understanding Christian doctrine. As a word of caution and encouragement, make the most of the screening process. Although some candidates may not currently qualify to serve as elders, through more discipline or training they may qualify in the future. Nurture, therefore, the spiritual development of men that show promise for future service as elders.

After satisfying the initial screening and questionnaire requirements, the nominee will meet with the presbytery or ordaining council. Initially, a pastor may need to call upon fellow pastors to comprise this group so that there is appropriate questioning of the candidates. Once elders are established, the presbytery will consist of the elders, and perhaps others in the congregation who are ordained with similar qualifications. A presbytery will need to read each nominee's questionnaire responses and pose questions related to the nominee's assurance, personal spiritual disciplines, understanding of doctrine, and views on the church. The rigor of the presbytery will help prepare the nominee for service as an elder, in which he will be called upon to answer the church's questions about doctrine and church life. The presbytery phase should never be mere formality, with an ordination service set following a brief time of questioning. Some issue might, in fact, be raised that will uncover questions about a man's family life or walk with Christ or views of the church. Disqualification must always be possible at any point during the screening process.

Once nominees have passed the initial screening, questionnaire, and presbytery, they are publicly identified to the church. The final line of screening involves the church. We give the congregation a two-week period to contest the nomination of any man deemed qualified for office of elder. Church members are asked to put in writing their concern and give this to the pastor, who will accompany the church member in discussing the concern with the nominee. If it is proved to be inconsequential, the nomination will stand. If the concern is warranted, then the nominee will be asked to withdraw his name from further consideration until the concern is resolved. After the two-week waiting period, the church is asked to approve the entire slate of elder nominees by vote or affirmation.

Hold the line on biblical standards throughout the entire process. The church body's level of respect will increase as they observe faithful adherence to the Scripture. Even after elders are established, the biblical standards must be reviewed regularly.

Ordain Elders

The ordination process gives both elders and congregation a chance to affirm God's hand upon leaders and people. Ordination as an elder implies that a man has been recognized as qualified for this biblical office, and set apart for faithful service. The church will be challenged to pray for the elders, hold them accountable, and follow their leadership. The elders will be challenged to faithfully teach the Word, give wise direction to the church, shepherd the flock of God, and set an example for all to follow. The ordination service provides a unique opportunity for showing the biblical foundation for the church's polity and how it affects the church.

Involve

New elders will need to be trained in how they are to function in regular church life. Training can take place during a special weekend retreat or even during the ongoing elders' meetings. Since the office of elder might be new to many in the congregation—including the new elders themselves—do not presume that new elders will understand fully the task before them. Training is essential.

Elders are to be involved in the full range of church life. Those elders who demonstrate pulpit gifts will be called upon to preach. Some elders will excel at pastoral care, others at administration, still others at leading worship. All will be involved in various areas of teaching. Some will be gifted in counseling and might need to take the lead in this area of church life. Those especially gifted in evangelism will need to be at the forefront of that part of church ministry. Since elders are shepherding the flock of God, all will need to consciously engage in discipling the church body. When it comes to solving problems, there is no better group in the church than the elders. It seems that the Lord of the church faithfully raises up men who work together in wisdom and discernment in applying Scripture to the difficult situations in church life.

As men serve together in the elder body, they will get a better feel for one another's gifts, strengths, and weaknesses. All will not teach equally well or be equally gifted in counseling or administration, so those whose gifts suit them for particular tasks will need to be directed to the areas where they can contribute most effectively.

Review

At least once a year the pastor should set forth the ministry of elders in his regular preaching schedule. The congregation—both new and longstanding members—needs to be reminded of the scriptural basis of elder leadership. Similarly, the elders themselves need the public challenge and accountability before the congregation in regard to what God expects of elders in Christian service.

REFLECTIONS

- What steps can you take to assess your church's present leadership?
- Do you recognize any men presently serving the church who appear to have the necessary qualifications to serve as elders?
- How can you communicate the need for plural eldership in your church?
- Identify a workable process in your own setting for selecting and screening elder candidates.

CHAPTER NINE

Putting It All Together

I'm accountable only to God," one pastor declared in response to those questioning some of his actions. Another pastor stated that the church elders, who had questioned some of his plans, had a responsibility to follow *his* vision for the church—without questions. Many, if not most, pastors would reject these kinds of brazen displays of autocratic authority. Yet the issue of authority regularly surfaces within congregations. Who holds authority within the church? In plural elder leadership within a congregational setting, the final authority in church matters resides in the congregation, yet elders are not without authority. For their oversight to follow the mandates of Scripture and impact the church, elders must exercise authority within the congregation.

ELDERS AND AUTHORITY

What kind of authority do elders hold within congregationalism? To correctly answer that question, it is crucial to understand the biblical teaching on the subject rather than simply to follow patterns of tradition. One church might place every decision affecting the church on the floor of a business meeting—and this happens quite often. Everything from decisions on carpeting the nursery to hiring a secretary to ordering a case of florescent bulbs to assisting someone with a benevolent need comes to the congregation's attention. This results in ill-informed congregations making decisions that affect the church's future. A single business meeting could involve the removal of a staff member, reduction in mission's giving, and the impulsive decision to build a new recreational facility. Can churches function like this? Certainly they can, albeit often at a snail's pace. More often, such functioning offends various groups within the church.

One would have to overlook, though, a number of New Testament passages to conclude that the congregation has no authority regarding church matters. In cases of discipline, the church body is the final arbiter for one's membership in the church (Matt. 18:15–20). While the elders might be involved in working through many of the details, the church decides whether to remove a member who has rejected biblical standards for Christian living or doctrine. In 1 Corinthians 5, Paul instructed the Corinthian church to stop tolerating a member's immoral behavior; instead, the church was to discipline the immoral member. The church took action, yet perhaps with too much severity (2 Cor. 2:5–11). In another instance of congregational authority, the church nominated qualified men to assist the apostles with food distribution (Acts 6:1–6). It appears, too, that Peter reported to the apostles *and* the church about carrying the gospel to the Gentiles, so that the whole group found satisfaction in his report (Acts 11:1–18). The church at Jerusalem sent Barnabas to investigate the spread of the gospel to Antioch, showing something of the church's involvement in missionary work (Acts 11:22; cf. 13:1–3 which offers similar implications). While the issues at the Jerusalem Council were first addressed to "the apostles and the elders" (Acts 15:6), the entire church got involved in the final decision that called for messengers to send a letter of acceptance and instruction for Gentile brethren (v. 22).

From these examples, we can conclude that the church was not a passive entity, watching apostles and elders from the sidelines. Members exercised authority through involvement in decision making that affected the future of the church.

But having noted this, however, there is also no doubt that a plural group led the church (cf. Acts 6:2 as the apostles called for congregational action; 15:6 as the apostles and elders "came together to look into this matter" of uncircumcised Gentles being converted; 20:17–35 as Paul instructed the elders of Ephesus to exercise spiritual oversight over that church, etc.). Congregationalism does not function well without effective, delegated leadership. And for leadership to be effective it must carry some level of authority.

Since Peter called for elders to shepherd the flock of God but to not lord this authority over them, it is obvious that delegated authority was involved (1 Peter 5:2–3). Shepherds do not normally offer suggestions to sheep! The church members are called upon to obey their leaders, even submit to them, because of their work of spiritual care (Heb. 13:17). Paul exhorts the Thessalonian church to "appreciate those who diligently labor among you, and have charge over you in the Lord and give you instruction" (1 Thess. 5:12). To "have charge over" clearly implies authority to lead the church. The church reciprocates with affection and esteem so that the leaders "are not to be regarded simply as the cold voice of authority."[1] The church needs leaders with authority in order to give the church direction, to exhort where needed, to correct and restore those who have gone astray, and to model the servant-leadership of Christ among the flock.

Because authority is delegated to the church's spiritual leaders, plural eldership demonstrates the wisdom of the Lord. "A plurality of elders is necessary because of the tendency of those in authority to play God."[2] The pastor who claimed he was accountable only to God is in "dangerous territory,"[3] and stands to make decisive errors in judgment that can affect his ministry and that of the church. Such pastors resist plural eldership because they do not want to be held accountable to anyone. The deceitfulness of the heart can trip up any pastor who has no regular, personal accountability for his time, actions, and lifestyle. Certainly he is accountable to the church for his actions, yet such accounting is often too vague to do any good. As John Hammett wisely pointed out, "To be accountable to the church is to be accountable to no one."[4] In other words, accountability to "the church" is too broad, and lacks the systematic interaction necessary to keep those in authority on track. So elder plurality holds each man—including the senior pastor as one of the elders—accountable to one another. Discussion of each man's spiritual development during elders' meetings or elders' retreats provides an atmosphere in which those with delegated authority understand the natural tendency to misuse authority. Accountability of this sort assures greater attention to the wise use of authority.

SENIOR PASTOR, ELDERS, AND AUTHORITY

I am thankful to have men around me who will not hesitate to exhort me, inquire about my priorities and schedule, or recommend that I take time off for refreshing. If I think that I'm slipping in the use of authority delegated to me as senior pastor, I counsel with my fellow elders, who enable me to see all sides of every issue. If I struggle over how I've handled a situation in the church, whether dealing with administration or personalities, my fellow elders, who share pastoral authority, help me to evaluate and resolve my concerns. So while I have ample authority within our church as the senior pastor and as an elder, I gladly share that authority lest my own weaknesses lead me to either abuse or neglect this authority.

Sometimes pastors ask how it is possible to function as a senior pastor with elders sharing pastoral authority and responsibility. Having had it both ways, I am convinced that the shared authority and responsibility in plural eldership works much better for the church as well as for me. Since every issue of church life no longer rests on my shoulders alone, I can concentrate on areas where I have the most to offer the church while my fellow elders do the same. When I have to make tough decisions affecting others within the church, I do not face these decisions alone, but I have godly men to pray for me and counsel me through the decisions. Times of decision are times of danger for men serving in a single pastoral authority position. Some issues cannot be thrown into open congregational discussion—initial disciplinary matters, for example, or problems with Sunday school teachers, restructuring church organizations, etc. But as elders meet in confidentiality, openly discussing each issue, searching the Scriptures for answers, and pleading together in prayer, a senior pastor can give more confident leadership to his church, knowing that decisions were made through the counsel of wise men.

I have been called to preach and love doing it. Because of my calling, I have more opportunity to address the congregation, and thus have a unique platform from which to exercise authority in the church. As the church's senior pastor, I am in a position to speak, to lead, and bring about change within the church. Although my authority is sometimes more noticeable due to my position, it is not above that of the other elders. Not all elders have this calling to preach, although all must be able to teach and exhort in doctrine. Yet all of us share in the authority of leading and giving oversight to the church. Some do so more behind the scenes, while others—such as the senior pastor—present more visibly the authority vested in plural elders. Mark Dever has expressed this well in an essay delivered at the 2004 *Issues in Baptist Polity* Conference in New Orleans.[5]

> The elder that we usually refer to as "the" pastor—the person like me—is, these days, the one who is generally set apart to fill the pulpit on Sunday. He is the one who marries and buries. He will often be paid—either part-time or fully. If the church is larger, he may be the one who hires and fires, and who sets the direction for the church as a whole. In our congregation in Washington, I am recognized as an elder by virtue of my call as the senior pastor of the church. Anyone whom we hire to work in ministry will either be called an assistant, or a pastor. The title pastor is reserved for those whom the congregation recognizes as an elder.
>
> Among these elders, I have only one vote. Because of the leadership responsibility I have as the main public teacher, there is undoubtedly a special degree of authority that attaches to my voice in elders' meetings, but the other brothers probably have by now a pretty good assessment of where I am most concerned and most helpful, and where I have less to contribute. In an eldership, though formal authority between the members is equal, there will always be those who garner special regard in one area or another.[6]

So what is the role of the senior pastor among plural eldership? First, he is devoted full-time to the work of ministry (although he may be full-time or part-time in employment). He spends major time in study, prayer, preparation, and engaging in times of proclamation and teaching. He likely has availed himself of specialized training that has equipped him for the responsibilities of serving as senior pastor.

Second, he is needed as a leader among the elders since he devotes his full labors and energies to the ministry. Quite practically, he is in the best position to lead, initiate policy, create changes, direct ministries, and give attention to the needs of the church body. He lives each day for this purpose, while some of the other elders might be involved in vocations such as sales or medicine or construction design, as is the case of our own church. The senior pastor's fellow elders support him as they recognize the priority of preaching in the New Testament ministry (1 Cor. 1–3). They also seek to sharpen and hone the senior pastor's skills and understanding of the Word through ongoing interaction.

Third, the distinct call to preach is not an equivalent to the office of elder. A church might have preachers who are not elders and elders who are not preachers, since the call to preach or ability to fill the pulpit is not required of elders. "There is no hint that all preachers must be presbyters [elders] or that all presbyters must be preachers."[7] Although others—whether elders or not—may preach occasionally (e.g., in the pastor's absence or to present a brief sermon series), there is no substitute for the senior pastor's dedication to the ongoing, systematic exposition of Holy Scripture, book by book. The need for consistent feeding of the flock of God in a carefully thought out fashion must not be undermined by routinely passing around pulpit responsibilities.

Finally, although the senior pastor has the major platform for addressing the church, he does so with the knowledge that his fellow elders stand with him in the work of ministry. A rogue pastor who would seek to speak *ex cathedra* as though he alone knows the will of God for the church will find plural eldership restrictive. While elders should appropriately encourage and commend the senior pastor in his labors, they should also kindly remind him of his own fallibility lest he think more highly of himself than he ought (Phil. 2:2–3; Rom. 12:3–5).

TWO OFFICES OR THREE?

One of the strongest objections to plural eldership comes from those who insist that non-preaching elders constitute a third office in the church, instead of the dual offices of pastor/elder/overseer and deacon. Obviously, through the centuries some have created three offices by artificially dividing the office of elder between "teaching elders" and "ruling elders." But Gerald Cowen states, "There is no such thing in the New Testament as an elder who only rules and does not teach."[8] Yet Cowen goes on to caricature plural eldership as a third office in the church and thus not scriptural. He goes so far as to identify the "pastor-elder-bishop" as only the preaching-pastor, writing, "No allowances are made for different kinds of elders with different qualifications. There is not one kind that is called of God to pastor and teach and another that is not."[9] In other words, if he is not called to serve as preaching-pastor of a church an elder has no business being an elder. Cowen even admits, "It is true that whenever the term *elder* or *bishop* is used in the New Testament it is used in the plural, which would mean that the general practice of the churches in New Testament times was to have at least two elders."[10] Yet since the New Testament does not set a precise number of "pastor-elders a church should have," Cowen bypasses plural eldership in favor of one called "the pastor,"[11] seemingly ignoring his own exegesis of the biblical texts.

Many of those making the strongest objections to plural elders would acknowledge multiple pastors in the church. There might be found in a given church a pastor of education, pastor of worship, pastor of students, pastor of children, pastor of administration, pastor of missions, pastor of evangelism, and even pastor of recreation! Certainly, not all of these pastors desire to be in the pulpit or are gifted to preach. Yet they are called pastors or associate pastors by the church. They do not fit the model of preaching-pastor, but are still called church "pastors"—plural. They are involved whenever the church needs a presbytery or ordination council to set apart men to the ministry or diaconate. They are expected to fulfill the qualifications noted in 1 Timothy 3 and Titus 1 for overseers and elders. But they have different gifts, different ministries, and different strengths for the total ministry of the church.

Cannot that same logic be applied to the plural eldership of both staff and non-staff members of the elders? While an elder might not be called or gifted to preach, he might be especially gifted at leading or organizing or administrating along with teaching. He contributes to the church in a different way than the senior pastor, offering strengths that the senior pastor might lack. Since there is no New Testament requirement that an elder must preach, then we have to conclude that given the other character qualities noted, if he is capable at teaching, then he is a good candidate to share the authority of leadership in the church.

CHURCH STAFF MEMBERS AS ELDERS

Some classify their church staff as elders and exclude non-staff members from the eldership. In this way the church is able to function with plurality of elders. But to exclude non-staff members from the eldership weakens the leadership group and deprives them of some of the most capable Christian servants in the church. It also places all leadership in the staff, which through departures due to accepting other calls or being removed from position can weaken the stability of long-term eldership in the church. The blend of pastoral staff and non-staff comprising the eldership offers more ownership in leading the church. Such a blend also provides balance from within the church and within the trained ministerial staff in better evaluating each issue from a variety of angles.

Should, however, every staff member automatically serve as an elder? While each staff member should meet the qualifications found in 1 Timothy 3 and Titus 1, it does not follow that each staff member should be an elder. On the other hand, several men in the congregation may, by the same biblical standards, be qualified to serve as elder, but do not serve in that office. It should not be assumed, then, that a staff member should be added to the eldership. He might be too young to offer the wise counsel necessary, still unproven through the crucible of difficult times, and thus lacking the insights of life experience that are so valuable in an elder.

During my college days I served as a staff member in two churches. At nineteen and twenty years old—and on staff—I was definitely not mature enough to exercise the authority of eldership! I did, however, have the ability to serve as a staff member, contributing to the overall work of ministry. But in decisions regarding doctrine and discipline, men who had longer track records of applying the Word of God to their lives were needed to lead the churches.

It appears best to have a balance between staff and non-staff elders, if at all possible. In this way, the staff cannot be charged with "stacking the deck" on votes of important issues, especially financial matters that affect the staff. If approved by the rest of the elders, it is beneficial for staff members to be part of elder meetings, to make their contributions, and to learn from the interaction. For a staff member to hold the title *elder*, though, is neither necessary nor most important, and if it does become "everything" to a staff member, that proves he is not ready to handle the mature responsibilities of eldership.

ELDERS AND DEACONS

Elders cannot do everything that needs to be accomplished in the church. Deacons serve in partnership with elders as the second of the two offices of the church, bearing particularly the load related to service in physical and temporal areas. Each church must work out its own details of how elders and deacons function, but at minimum, these two offices should seek to complement each other rather than to compete. Their duties might occasionally overlap, and in such times they should communicate well with each other and realize how their service together meets the leadership needs in the church.

A strong deacon body lays the groundwork for effective elders, allowing elders to focus on their particular responsibilities while the deacons relieve them from necessary but mundane tasks. One area in which our deacons and elders have found effective partnership is in caring for the members of the body. Each deacon is assigned a number of church families for whom he is responsible, contacting them, praying for them, and watching over them. He will alert the elders if problems with a family warrant special concern. Families are also assigned to each of our elders so that elders overlap with the deacons in church family care. These assignments help us to maximize contacts with individuals, and minimize the danger of allowing anyone to "slip through the cracks." To help with accountability in this area, deacons and elders maintain their own contact journal, in which they make notes of the varied contacts they have in the body and particular needs requiring more attention. The deacons meet with our elders on a monthly basis to discuss our contacts with family members, make known any physical or spiritual need, identify those who have grown slack in church attendance, and pray for church family needs. In this way our deacons partner with the elders in the work of ministry.

The elders and deacons might take part in the committees of the church, perhaps even having one or the other assigned to each committee. Our elders nominate all committee members and decide which committees are needed each year in order adequately to serve the church. With few exceptions, each committee has at least one elder or deacon. Since these men are most aware of the direction of the church, they help the committees remain focused on how to best utilize the gifts of the church, thus maintaining continuity in the overall work of the church.

ELDERS' MEETINGS

Our elders meet on a monthly basis, but also maintain regular contact with each other through e-mail and telephone conversations. We serve together, but we are also friends who pray for each other and hold each other accountable in our Christian walks. Meetings are planned to best utilize our time together and to consider the most necessary areas of church needs. Below is a recent agenda from one of our elders' meetings (our deacons attended the first part of the meeting).

- Scripture reading and prayer
- Review contacts with members, identifying needs or additional contacts needed
- Deacons identify a Spring Work Day
- Discuss future elder and deacon selection for 2004
- *Deacons dismissed*
- Plan Wednesday night schedule for the summer; discuss small groups and agenda
- Plan Sunday school studies for the summer and fall
- Discuss replacement for a children's class on Wednesday nights

- Organize membership interviews
- Discuss ongoing pastoral internships; review request for internship
- Discuss evangelistic outreach ideas for summer and fall

I must admit that sometimes we do not complete the agenda. If not, we might meet an additional time or carry on some of our discussion via e-mail. When we bring on new elders we add training to the agenda in order to introduce the new elders to the ministry of elders. We have found that a two- to three-hour period sometimes is not enough to pray, discuss church family needs, deal with issues of discipline, and make plans for the church. So we might plan a retreat in order to concentrate time on pressing matters or the larger planning issues of the church. In our times together we've learned to value openness, forthrightness, gentleness, and humility.

ELDERS AND CONGREGATIONAL MEETINGS

In Baptist church life, business meetings often leave carnage behind. I have rarely met a Baptist pastor or long-time church member who does not have war stories to tell about business meetings. But such should never be the case when the Spirit-indwelled, regularly-disciplined, regenerate membership of a local church assemble to discuss membership issues. Plural eldership, however, covers much of the business that would often otherwise be discussed by the congregation, who, for the most part, might be uninformed. If a church trusts its elders as men of God who serve for the good of the church, the majority of issues that concern the local church need not be a subject for discussion in monthly business meetings. Certainly the membership at large should be consulted on major issues such as calling staff members to serve or buying property or building projects or major changes to church structure. But elders and deacons work together in plural leadership to address the regular business of church life—elders concentrating on the spiritual, and deacons concentrating on the temporal—so that the church body can concentrate on the work of ministry.

Each church will need to develop a timeframe suitable for congregational meetings. Monthly meetings are largely unnecessary, but some type of monthly communication from the elders and deacons—keeping the congregation up-to-date on the latest changes, decisions, and needs—might prove to solidify the church's harmony. Some churches have found that quarterly meetings or bi-yearly meetings work well. Others opt for a yearly congregational meeting that considers the church budget and recommendations for the year ahead. If a church has been accustomed to monthly business meetings that wade through endless details, then a pastor would be wise to slowly taper this kind of tradition rather than abruptly end it.

At times, of course, the congregation should be called into corporate action. Accepting new members or dismissing from membership those who have moved or requested a membership transfer, call for brief congregational meetings. In addressing disciplinary matters, we have followed the practice of addressing them during the church's gathering at the Lord's Supper. Such timing seems appropriate considering the sanctity of the service as a *church* ordinance that acknowledges the person and work of Christ, and the effect of His work upon the entire church body. One of the privileges of church membership is admission to the Lord's Table, so to deny this privilege due to matters of church discipline requires that the church unite to publicly express its censure of the erring party.

ELDERS' TERMS OF SERVICE AND DISMISSAL

While the New Testament affirms plural eldership it does not establish the precise number that constitutes plurality or how long each elder is to serve. The polity framework sketched in the New Testament does not give every detail; rather, it leaves some things to the wisdom of the local churches. It would be inadvisable, for example, to establish a rotating system of elders unless the size and maturity of the church membership ensures an adequate number of elders to maintain plurality. Rotation has its pluses, in that more men will be able to serve the church, and the elder body will maintain more diversity. But rotation assumes that, each year, mature, qualified men will be ready to join the elder body for service. If true, rotation can be a healthy decision for the church in providing "fresh troops" to the demanding role of elders. Rotation, though, also assumes a set quota for the elder body that must be met each year during the selection process.

A disadvantage to rotation is that wise, mature leaders who understand the church's needs rotate out of active service. That can be a great loss to the church. Rotation, as stated above, establishes a quota to fill with the required number of elders, even if the church lacks qualified men to serve. Filling spots with unqualified men can weaken the effectiveness of the entire elder body, especially if biblical standards are compromised simply to fill a quota.

Perhaps a better way to address term length—particularly in churches that have previously grown accustomed to a rotating deacon body—is to begin with elders serving an unspecified length, with the caveat that a review of rotation and tenure will take place three or five years after beginning plural elder leadership. Elders' tenure can be reviewed as part of reexamining the church's governing documents (constitution, bylaws, polity manual, etc.). It would be wise to include some men outside of the elder body to assist in this review and offer objective thoughts about any changes.

The only New Testament passage addressing the removal of elders relates to church discipline: "Do not receive an accusation against an elder except on the basis of two or three witnesses" (1 Tim. 5:19). Since elders are open to congregational scrutiny, and at times baseless accusations, Paul adopts the Old Testament practice requiring two or three witnesses to substantiate an accusation of serious offense (Deut. 19:15). "None are more exposed to slanders and insults," wrote John Calvin, "than godly teachers. They may perform their duties correctly and conscientiously, yet 'they never avoid a thousand criticisms.'"[12] Paul does not specify what type of sin falls into this category, but it can be assumed that it is serious enough to call into question the elder's capacity to continue serving the church. Paul further states the high accountability that an elder must maintain to his office and the trust of the church: "Those who continue in sin, rebuke in the presence of all, so that the rest also will be fearful of sinning" (1 Tim. 5:20). If an accused elder continues in sin, the church must take action to reestablish the testimony of the elders and the church. Since one of the four primary responsibilities of elders is to model the Christian life, breaking this trust by continual sin leads to a public rebuke of the elder before the congregation. The term for *rebuke* implies that the charges of sin have been clearly substantiated and the elder found guilty. Although the text does not give the details, there is little doubt that the convicted elder is removed from office in the same way that a church member would, as an act of discipline, be censured and removed from active membership. It would make no sense for him to continue serving after such public rebuke of his folly. As Albert Mohler stated, "Clearly, leadership carries a higher burden, and the sins of an elder cause an even greater injury to the church. The public rebuke is necessary, for the elder sins against the entire congregation."[13]

ELDERS: NOW, LATER, OR NEVER

The biblical teaching on plural eldership having now been investigated, and recommendations offered for establishing elder leadership in churches, the final hurdle is determining the appropriate response. Some who study the subject of elders declare that they will *never* consider it for their church polity. Some traditions are deeply ingrained and some interpretations of New Testament polity differ from what has been presented here. In such cases, consider the following exhortation: Whatever type of leadership structure you embrace, by all means determine to raise the standards for leaders to match the biblical requirements. Failure of leaders to meet those requirements is the greatest deficiency in church leadership! A lack of godly men, saturated in the Scriptures, wise through the application of God's Word to daily life, and faithful in spiritual disciplines leaves any leadership structure deficient. So if plural elder leadership does not match your views of polity, at least give major attention to elevating standards to mirror the biblical demands on spiritual leaders.

Perhaps while reading this book you have determined to begin plural elder leadership in your own church. You are ready to do it *now!* Not so fast, please. Remember to lay the groundwork. Radical changes in church polity might not find a welcome reception, so proceed judiciously. The previous chapter offers a model for bringing about the change in congregational thinking and implementing the transition to elder leadership. Study it carefully, adapt it to your own setting, and by God's grace, move forward.

Some of you may find plural elder leadership appealing—yet your tenure at your church has been brief and you do not want it to quickly end. So you are pondering the idea of making a change in your church structure *later*. Then get started *now*. Focus on faithfully teaching the Scripture to your church, because more important than changing your polity is developing a congregation that studies and applies the Word to daily life. Set your focus, by God's grace, on developing just such a church. The polity change will follow in due time, because the congregation that loves the Word of God and desires to follow whatever the Lord has spoken will be open to plural eldership. Keep challenging your church to study the Scriptures thoroughly, to ask questions of the biblical texts, and to think biblically.

Changing church polity to align with the teaching of the New Testament can be a fascinating journey. At times the journey will take on a Daniel Boone-esque appearance, as you hack your way through the underbrush that has covered the clear paths of God's revelation. On other occasions you might feel as though you are in a hot air balloon, rising to great heights in the church's grasp of Scripture, only to suddenly sink as you strive for distinct changes demanded in the Word. Stay on the journey, knowing that the Lord of the church will one day call for you to report on how faithfully you discharged your duties to His flock. And maybe along the journey, you will know the joy of leading your church to embrace plural elder leadership. Then, a new phase of the journey begins!

REFLECTIONS

- Think about the subject of authority in the church. How would you characterize the authority of the congregation and the authority of the elders? In what ways does this authority differ?
- How can the senior pastor function with elders who share equal authority?
- How do the elders and deacons cooperate in service for the good of the church?
- What is your response to this study of plural elder leadership? In what ways does this challenge your previous thoughts about church polity?

Endnotes

FOREWORD

1. See 1 Thessalonians 5 and 2 Thessalonians 2 for some early words of Paul on this great reality.
2. I've written a short booklet that addresses this concern head-on. Mark Dever, *Baptists and Elders* (Washington, D.C.: 9 Marks Ministries, 2005). Also, see three other resources on this point. For a simple summary of the Bible's teaching on this, see Mark Dever, *Nine Marks of a Healthy Church* 2d ed. (Wheaton: Crossway, 2004). For a look at these ideas in Baptist History, see Mark Dever, ed., *Polity* (Washington, D.C.: 9 Marks Ministries, 2001). And for a consideration of how plural eldership works out in practice, see Mark Dever, *A Display of God's Glory* (Washington, D.C.: 9 Marks Ministries, 2001).
3. John MacArthur Jr., *Answering the Key Questions About Elders* (Panorama City, Calif.: Grace to You, 1984).

CHAPTER 1: WHY "BAPTIST ELDERS" IS NOT AN OXYMORON

1. Boyce Broadus, *Baptists of Russellville, Alabama, 1867–1967* (Birmingham, Ala.: Banner Press, 1967), 3. Miss Broadus was the granddaughter of noted Southern Baptist theologian John Broadus.
2. Gregory A. Wills, *Democratic Religion: Freedom, Authority, and Church Discipline in the Baptist South, 1785–1900* (New York: Oxford University Press,

1997), 51, 155 n. 4. Wills derives this conclusion from several eighteenth- and nineteenth-century historical records of Baptists in Georgia.

3. J. H. Grimes, *History of Middle Tennessee Baptists* (Nashville: Baptist and Reflector, 1902), 158.

4. Ibid. Admittedly, the terms *ruling elders* and *lay elders* are not New Testament titles. The distinction in these titles resembles, however, some of the common titles used in modern churches, e.g., *senior* pastor, *associate* pastor, pastor of *education,* and *executive* pastor. All are considered to be serving in pastoral roles but not all have the same function within the local church setting. The adjective qualifies the role just as it has done with the *ruling* elder and *lay* elder titles. I'm indebted to Dr. Daniel Akin for raising questions about this impor- tant historical distinction (personal correspondence, July 24, 2003).

5. David Benedict, *General History of the Baptist Denomination in America and Other Parts of the World* (Boston: Manning and Loring, 1813), 176.

6. Wills, *Democratic Religion,* 31, identifies Silas Mercer in Georgia and Isaac Backus of Massachusetts as "Revolutionary War-era leaders" among Baptists. So Tinsley's service in plural eldership took place within a prominent church.

7. A. D. Gillette, ed., *Minutes of the Philadelphia Baptist Association 1707– 1807: Being the First One Hundred Years of Its Existence* (1851; repr., Spring- field, Mo.: Particular Baptist Press, 2002), 39.

8. Ibid., 102.

9. Greg Wills, "The Church: Baptists and Their Churches in the Eighteenth and Nineteenth Centuries," in *Polity: Biblical Arguments on How to Con- duct Church Life,* ed. Mark Dever (Washington, D.C.: Center for Church Reform, 2001), 33–35.

10. Ibid., 34. Wills summarizes Johnson's view.

11. My use of *lay elders* by way of explaining the historical practice of plural eldership is not necessarily an endorsement of the term for modern usage. A better distinction, when necessary for explanation, might be *non-staff elders* serving with the elders that constitute the church staff. This assumes that, unlike staff elders, the non-staff elders receive no compensation from the church for their service.

12. A. C. Underwood, *A History of the English Baptists* (London: Carey Kingsgate Press, 1947), 130–31.

13. James M. Renihan, "The Practical Ecclesiology of the English Particular Baptists, 1675–1705: The Doctrine of the Church in the Second London Baptist Confession as Implemented in the Subscribing Churches" (Ph.D. diss., Trinity Evangelical Divinity School, 1997), 196.

14. Ibid., 201.
15. Benjamin Keach, *The Glory of a True Church and Its Discipline Display'd* (London: n.p., 1697), 15–16 (emphasis Keach), quoted in Renihan, "Practical Ecclesiology," 202.
16. Renihan, "Practical Ecclesiology," 203.
17. Ibid., 205.
18. Ibid., 210, summarizing Coxe's comments.
19. Ibid., 210; quoting Hanserd Knollys, *The Word That Now Is* (London: Tho. Snowden, 1681), 52.
20. John Piper, *Biblical Eldership: Shepherd the Flock of God Among You*, app. 1, http://www.desiringgod.org/library/tbi/bib_eldership.html. (accessed March 29. 2003). See also John Piper, *Biblical Eldership* (Minneapolis: Desiring God Ministries, 1999).
21. Philip Schaff, *The Creeds of Christendom with a History and Critical Notes: The Evangelical Protestant Creeds with Translations*, ed. and rev. David Schaff, 6th ed. (Grand Rapids: Baker, 1993), 3:725.
22. Ibid., 739.
23. Ibid., 747.
24. Paul Burleson in a sermon, "An Historical Study of Baptist Elders—1 Peter 5:14," at Trinity Baptist Church in Norman, Oklahoma (http://www.hhbc.com/webpages/baptist1.htm), 2 (accessed Nov. 21, 2002), offers three reasons for the decline of elders in Baptist life in the late 1800s to 1900s. First, in the expansion of Baptist churches into the west, the single pastor/church planter often served as a circuit riding minister, handling the bulk of church duties with plural eldership fading in the process. Presumably, qualified male leadership was scarce in the early days. Second, the rise of Landmarkism, with its emphasis on "democratic rule with no elder rule" had profound influence on Southern Baptist life and practice. Third, "the rise of the Campbelites"—now called the Church of Christ, who "used the word elder exclusively"—caused Baptists to react and reject the name *elder*, using only the word *pastor* for those involved in church ministry and leadership.
25. I'm indebted to Shawn Wright, at the Southern Baptist Theological Seminary in Louisville, Kentucky, for research and comments that helped to clarify this point (personal correspondence, January 24, 2003).
26. Benjamin Griffith, "A Short Treatise Concerning a True and Orderly Gospel Church" (Philadelphia: Philadelphia Baptist Association, 1743), quoted in Mark Dever, ed., *Polity: Biblical Arguments on How to Conduct Church Life* (Washington, D.C.: Center for Church Reform, 2001), 98.

27. Ibid.

28. Ibid.

29. W. B. Johnson, "The Gospel Developed through the Government and Order of the Churches of Jesus Christ" (Richmond: H. K. Ellyson, 1846), quoted in Dever, *Polity*, 193.

30. Ibid., 192–93.

31. Ibid., 191.

32. Ibid., 194.

33. Ibid., 196–97.

34. Piper, *Biblical Eldership*, app. 1.

CHAPTER 2: ELDERS IN THE NEW TESTAMENT

1. See John Piper, *Brothers, We Are Not Professionals!* (Nashville: Broadman and Holman, 2002).

2. The elder permeated everyday life during the New Testament era. For example, ancient Sparta applied the term to those who governed their communities, as well as to decision-makers in academic circles. The Greeks, unlike the Jews, did not necessarily factor age into their usage of the term. Those considered elders in ancient Israel held responsibility for political, military, and even judicial matters. But when the times of kings arose, elders were replaced with the royal bureaucracy (G. Bornkamm, "Presbuteros," in *Theological Dictionary of the New Testament*, ed. Gerhard Kittel, trans. Geoffrey Bromiley [Grand Rapids: Eerdmans, 1968], 6:652–57 [hereafter cited as *TDNT*]).

3. G. Bornkamm, "Presbuteros," in *TDNT*, 6:664.

4. Walter Bauer, W. Arndt, and F. W. Gingrich, *A Greek-English Lexicon of the New Testament and Other Early Christianity Literature* (Chicago: The University of Chicago Press, 1957), 299 (hereafter cited as BAG).

5. H. Beyer, "Episkopos," in *TDNT*, 2:600–1.

6. Ibid., 610–11.

7. J. Jeremias, "Poimane," in *TDNT*, 6:486.

8. BAG, 690.

9. Personal correspondence with Bill Murray, Germantown, Tennessee, September 12, 2002.

10. Wayne Grudem, *Systematic Theology: An Introduction to Biblical Doctrine* (Grand Rapids: Zondervan, 1994), 913.

11. See D. Martyn Lloyd-Jones, *Preaching and Preachers* (Grand Rapids: Zondervan, 1975), 100–20; Tony Sargent, *The Sacred Anointing: The Preaching of Dr. Martyn Lloyd-Jones* (Wheaton, Ill.: Crossway, 1994), 17–38.

12. See 1 Timothy 3:2, where teaching refers to instruction in biblical doc-
    trines, and Titus 1:9, where the exhortations or urgings are to be grounded
    in Scripture, as are the refutations.
13. Mark Dever, *A Display of God's Glory: Basics of Church Structure* (Wash-
    ington, D.C.: Center for Church Reform, 2001), 24.
14. Fritz Rienecker and Cleon Rogers, *Linguistic Key to the Greek New Testa-
    ment* (Grand Rapids: Zondervan, 1980), 631.
15. John Piper, *Biblical Eldership: Shepherd the Flock of God Among You*, sec. 6,
    http://www.desiringgod.org/library/tbi/bib_eldership.html. (accessed
    March 25, 2003). See also John Piper, *Biblical Eldership* (Minneapolis: De-
    siring God Ministries, 1999).
16. Grudem, *Systematic Theology,* 916.
17. See Mark Dever, *Nine Marks of a Healthy Church* (Wheaton, Ill.: Crossway,
    2000), 153–79.
18. Rienecker and Rogers, *Linguistic Key,* 602.
19. BAG, 713.
20. This is clearly stated in Acts 20:28: "Be on guard for yourselves and for all
    the flock, among which the Holy Spirit has made you overseers, to *shep-
    herd the church of God* which He purchased with His own blood," and in 1
    Peter 5:2: "*Shepherd the flock of God* among you" (italics added).

CHAPTER 3: CHARACTER AND CONGREGATIONALISM

1. Daniel Wallace, "Who Should Run the Church? A Case for the Plurality of
   Elders," 7, http://www.bible.org/docs/soapbox/caseform.htm. (accessed
   March 25, 2003).
2. Fritz Rienecker and Cleon Rogers, *Linguistic Key to the Greek New Testament* (Grand Rapids: Zondervan, 1980), 297.
3. BAG, *episkeptomai,* 298.
4. John Piper, *Biblical Eldership: Shepherd the Flock of God Among You*, sec. 4,
   principle 9, http://www.desiringgod.org/library/tbi/bib_eldership.html.
   (accessed March 25, 2003). See also John Piper, *Biblical Eldership* (Minneapolis: Desiring God Ministries, 1999).
5. Gerald Cowen, *Who Rules the Church? Examining Congregational Leadership
   and Church Government* (Nashville: Broadman and Holman, 2003), 63.
6. Italics added, where *must* implies a moral necessity.
7. John MacArthur, *Shepherdology: A Master Plan for Church Leadership* (Panorama City, Calif.: Master's Fellowship, 1989), 72.
8. Piper, *Biblical Eldership,* sec. 7.

9. Ibid.

10. Rienecker and Rogers, *Linguistic Key,* 622.

11. Piper, *Biblical Eldership,* sec. 7.

12. Ibid.

13. Rienecker and Rogers, *Linguistic Key,* 652.

14. Ibid.

15. Alexander Strauch, *Biblical Eldership: An Urgent Call to Restore Biblical Church Leadership,* rev. and exp. (Littleton, Colo.: Lewis and Roth, 1995), 114.

16. Quoted in Robert Wring, "An Examination of the Practice of Elder Rule in Selected Southern Baptist Churches in the Light of New Testament Teaching" (Ph.D. diss., Mid-America Baptist Theological Seminary, 2002), 96–97.

17. Rienecker and Rogers, *Linguistic Key,* 299–300.

18. Mark Dever, *Nine Marks of a Healthy Church* (Wheaton, Ill.: Crossway, 2000), 212.

19. Piper, *Biblical Eldership,* sec. 4, principle 2.

20. Ibid., sec. 4, principle 3.

21. Timothy and Denise George, eds., *John A. Broadus: Baptist Confessions, Covenants, and Catechisms* (Nashville: Broadman and Holman Publishers, 1996), 86.

22. Wallace, "Who Should Run the Church?" 6 (italics in original).

CHAPTER 4: A MODEL FOR OUR TIMES

1. See Philip Schaff, *The Creeds of Christendom with a History and Critical Notes: The Evangelical Protestant Creeds with Translations,* ed. and rev. David Schaff, 6th ed. (Grand Rapids: Baker, 1993), 3:738–40, 747.

2. Robert Wring, "An Examination of the Practice of Elder Rule in Selected Southern Baptist Churches in the Light of New Testament Teaching" (Ph.D. diss., Mid-America Baptist Theological Seminary, 2002), 52.

3. John MacArthur, *The Master's Plan for the Church* (Chicago: Moody, 1991), 195.

4. Curtis Vaughan, *Founders Study Guide Commentary: Ephesians* (Cape Coral, Fla.: Founders Press, 2002), 15.

5. Ibid., 15.

6. Even if, as some conjecture, multiple house churches did exist, the fact remains that they were united as part of one church with plural elders serving the pastoral needs.

7. BAG, 690, explains that the symbol of a shepherd leading, guiding, and

ruling is in mind, and in this case refers to "the administration of a congregation."

8. See chapter 6 for a detailed look at this text.

9. See Justo L. Gonzalez, *The Story of Christianity: The Early Church to Present Day* (Peabody, Mass.: Prince Press, 2001), 31–108.

10. Fritz Rienecker and Cleon Rogers, *Linguistic Key to the Greek New Testament* (Grand Rapids: Zondervan, 1980), 318

11. John Piper, *Brothers, We Are Not Professionals! A Plea to Pastors for Radical Ministry* (Nashville: Broadman and Holman, 2002), 1.

12. John Stott, *The Spirit, the Church, and the World: The Message of Acts* (Downers Grove, Ill.: InterVarsity, 1990), 327.

13. Richard Baxter, *The Reformed Pastor: A Pattern for Personal Growth and Ministry* (Portland, Ore.: Multnomah, 1982, based on 1830 edition), 27–32.

14. Fred Malone, "Do Personal Work," in *Dear Timothy: Letters on Pastoral Ministry*, ed. Thomas K. Ascol (Cape Coral, Fla.: Founders Press, 2004), 179.

15. Charles Bridges, *The Christian Ministry: with an Inquiry into the Causes of its Inefficiency* (1830; repr., Carlisle, Pa.: Banner of Truth, 1991), 344.

16. Ibid.

17. J. Oswald Sanders, *Spiritual Leadership* (Chicago: Moody, 1980), 40, quoted in John MacArthur, *Shepherdology: A Master Plan for Church Leadership* (Panorama City, Calif.: Master's Fellowship, 1989), 134.

18. John Murray, *The Collected Writings of John Murray: The Claims of Truth*, (Edinburgh: Banner of Truth Trust, 1976), 1:265–66.

19. BAG, 546.

20. Stott, *The Spirit, the Church, and the World*, 329.

21. A *presbytery* refers to an assembled body of elders.

22. Stott, *The Spirit, the Church, and the World*, 329.

CHAPTER 5: ELDERS AND CONGREGATION IN CONCERT

1. Philip Edgcumbe Hughes, *A Commentary on the Epistle to the Hebrews* (Grand Rapids: Eerdmans, 1977), 1.

2. Andrew H. Trotter Jr., *Guides to New Testament Exegesis: Interpreting the Epistle to the Hebrews* (Grand Rapids: Baker, 1997), 45.

3. Ibid.

4. Ibid., 47.

5. Ibid., 37–38.

6. Ibid., 38.

7. BAG, 344. The word *ēgeomai*, when used in the present participle, will be translated as "ruler, leader," with the context determining the particular type leader identified. The men accompanying Paul and Barnabas with the Jerusalem Council letter, Judas called Barsabbas and Silas, are in Acts 15:22 called "leading men among the brethren." The same is used of Paul in Acts 14:12, where the participle is used in noun form, "the leader of the talk," according to Fritz Rienecker and Cleon Rogers, *Linguistic Key to the Greek New Testament* (Grand Rapids: Zondervan, 1980), 296. It seems that the present participle of *egeomai* took on almost technical meaning with the idea that leadership involved speaking or discoursing of some type. I would argue that this is the usage in Hebrews 13:7, 17, since the implication is that these leaders "spoke the word of God to you" and watched over the souls of the congregation—indicating that *egeomai* is a distinctly pastoral term that includes teaching, instruction, and preaching.

8. The Greek word *agrupnousin* means "to be without sleep, to seek after sleep, to be watchful," according to Rienecker and Rogers, *Linguistic Key*, 720, and "to keep watch over something, guard, care for it," according to BAG, 14.

9. BAG, 902, the Greek term is *psuchē*.

10. David F. Wells, *No Place for Truth: Or Whatever Happened to Evangelical Theology?* (Grand Rapids: Eerdmans, 1993), 106.

11. See my essay, "The Pastor and Church Growth: How to Deal with the Modern Problem of Pragmatism," in *Reforming Pastoral Ministry: Challenges for Ministry in Postmodern Times,* ed. John Armstrong (Wheaton, Ill.: Crossway, 2001), 263ff.; and John MacArthur Jr., *Ashamed of the Gospel: When the Church Becomes Like the World* (Wheaton, Ill.: Crossway, 1993).

12. Wells, *No Place for Truth,* 108 (author's italics).

13. D. Edmund Hiebert, *The Epistles of John: An Expositional Commentary* (Greenville, S.C.: Bob Jones University Press, 1991), 336.

14. P. H. Mell, *Corrective Church Discipline with a Development of the Scriptural Principles upon which It Is Based* (Charleston, S.C.: Southern Baptist Publication Society, 1860), quoted in Mark Dever, ed., *Polity: Biblical Arguments on How to Conduct Church Life* (Washington, D.C.: Center for Church Reform, 2001), 423.

15. I'm indebted to one of my fellow elders, Tom Tollett, in pointing out this implication from the text.

16. Hughes, *Commentary on the Epistle to the Hebrews,* 586.

17. Ibid., 587.

18. "When one exhorts others to participate with him in any act or condition, the subjunctive is used in the first person plural," known as the hortatory subjunctive, according to H. E. Dana and Julius Mantey, *A Manual Grammar of the Greek New Testament* (Toronto: Macmillan, 1957), 171.

19. John Owen, *The Works of John Owen: Temptation and Sin* (Carlisle, Pa.: Banner of Truth Trust, 1991), 6:96, explains temptation as *"any thing, state, way, or condition that, upon any account whatever, hath a force or efficacy to seduce, to draw the mind and heart of a man from its obedience, which God requires of him, into any sin, in any degree of it whatever."* He further points out that particular temptation is that "which causes or occasions him to sin, or in any thing to go off from his duty, either by *bringing* evil into his heart, or *drawing* out that evil that is in his heart, or any other way diverting him from communion with God, and that constant, equal, universal obedience, in matter and manner, that is required of him."

20. Hughes, *Commentary on the Epistle to the Hebrews,* 410.

21. Ibid., 414.

22. Ibid., 415.

23. Rienecker and Rogers explain the word *stimulate (paroxusmos)* to mean "irritating, inciting, stimulation" (*Linguistic Key,* 703). It leaves no question concerning the active involvement of each church member in helping to motivate others in the body toward faithful Christian service.

24. Philip Ryken, *City on a Hill: Reclaiming the Biblical Pattern for the Church in the Twenty-first Century* (Chicago: Moody, 2003), 97–98.

25. Ibid., 98.

26. Ibid.

27. Ibid., 101.

28. J. P. Migne, ed. Patrologia Graeca, "Chrysostom," vol. 63 (London: ET, 1893), quoted in Hughes, *Commentary on the Epistle to the Hebrews,* 585–86.

29. By this it is to be inferred that elders are not involved in soliciting bank or investment statements. Elders may, however, find occasions to exhort members regarding giving if negligence in this area has taken place, or regarding wise budgeting if warranted.

30. Raymond Brown, *The Bible Speaks Today: the Message of Hebrews* (Downers Grove, Ill.: InterVarsity, 1982), 264.

31. Ibid., 264–65.

32. Alexander Strauch, *Biblical Eldership: An Urgent Call to Restore Biblical Church Leadership,* rev. and exp. (Littleton, Colo.: Lewis and Roth, 1995), 160.

33. John MacArthur, *MacArthur's New Testament Commentaries: Hebrews* (Chicago: Moody, 1983), 446.

34. Brown, *Bible Speaks Today,* 265.

35. Rienecker and Rogers, *Linguistic Key,* 720.

36. R. Kent Hughes, *Preaching the Word: Hebrews, an Anchor for the Soul* (Wheaton, Ill.: Crossway, 1993), 2:239.

CHAPTER 6: SPIRITUAL LEADERS FOR GOD'S FLOCK

1. Mark Dever, *Nine Marks of a Healthy Church* (Wheaton, Ill.: Crossway, 2000), 20.

2. Robert G. Torbet, *A History of the Baptists,* 3d ed. (Valley Forge, Pa.: Judson, 1975), 253.

3. Ibid., 244.

4. Dever, *Nine Marks,* 20.

5. Daryl C. Cornett, "Baptist Ecclesiology: A Faithful Application of New Testament Principles," *Journal for Baptist Theology and Ministry* 2, no. 1 (Spring 2004): 30.

6. W. B. Johnson, *The Gospel Developed Through the Government and Order of the Churches of Jesus Christ* (n.p., 1846); quoted in Mark Dever, ed., *Polity: Biblical Arguments on How to Conduct Church Life* (Washington, D.C.: Center for Church Reform, 2001), 193.

7. Robert Leighton, *An Obedient and Patient Faith: An Exposition of 1 Peter* (1853; repr., Amityville, N.Y.: Calvary Press, 1995), 437.

8. Paul J. Achtemeier, *1 Peter,* Hermeneia: A Critical and Historical Commentary on the Bible (Minneapolis: Fortress Press, 1996), 23–34.

9. Ibid., 28–29.

10. "It is the title of an office rather than a description of seniority." Peter H. Davids, *The First Epistle of Peter,* The New International Commentary on the New Testament (Grand Rapids: Eerdmans, 1990), 175.

11. See chapter 4 for additional discussion on this passage.

12. Johnson, *The Gospel Developed,* quoted in Dever, *Polity,* 194.

13. The most obvious example is the Jerusalem Council in Acts 15, but consider also Acts 11:1–18, Peter's testimony before the leaders of the church, as well as Acts 11:19–26, the action of the church leaders in response to the spread of the gospel to Antioch.

14. Fritz Rienecker and Cleon Rogers, *Linguistic Key to the Greek New Testament* (Grand Rapids: Zondervan, 1980), 765, states that the term *koinonos* means "partner, sharer."

15. Compare the verb *poimainō,* translated as "to shepherd" as used here with the noun *poimēn,* which is translated as "pastor" in Ephesians 4:11; also *episkopountes,* "exercising oversight," used as a verb with the noun *episkopos,* translated as "overseer." See BAG, 298–99, 690.

16. John Calvin, *Calvin's Commentaries: Commentaries on the Catholic Epistles,* (repr., Grand Rapids: Baker, 1999), 22:144.

17. J. H. Jowett, *The Epistles of Peter* (1905; repr., Grand Rapids: Kregel, 1993), 96.

18. For additional insight on this work of elders as shepherds, see Richard L. Mayhue, "Watching and Warning," in *Rediscovering Pastoral Ministry: Shaping Contemporary Ministry with Biblical Mandates,* ed. John MacArthur Jr. (Dallas: Word, 1995), 336–50; John MacArthur Jr., "Shepherding the Flock of God," in *The Master's Plan for the Church* (Chicago: Moody, 1991), 169–76; Philip Graham Ryken, "Shepherding God's Flock: Pastoral Care," in *City on a Hill: Reclaiming the Biblical Pattern for the Church in the Twenty-first Century* (Chicago: Moody, 2003), 93–110.

19. Rienecker and Rogers, *Linguistic Key,* 765.

20. Peter Jeffreys, *Living for Christ in a Pagan World: 1 and 2 Peter Simply Explained* (Durham, England: Evangelical Press, 1990), 161–62.

21. "The word is extremely strong and expresses enthusiasm and devoted zeal" (Rienecker and Rogers, *Linguistic Key,* 765).

22. Leighton, *Obedient and Patient Faith,* 469, refers to the Medieval preacher Bernard's comment, "Had I some of that blood poured forth on the cross, how carefully would I carry it! And ought I not be as careful of those souls that it was shed for?"

23. Davids, *The First Epistle of Peter,* 183, identifies some that hold the "younger" to "a particular class or group in the church that needed to be subject to the official leadership," following the French scholar Spicq. Another scholar, K. H. Schelkle, citing Polycarp, "simply points out that youth often struggle with leadership."

24. Ibid., 184.

25. Ibid.

26. Rienecker and Rogers, *Linguistic Key,* 765.

27. Achtemeier, *1 Peter,* 324–25. He also identifies a number of Old Testament passages showing the shepherd motif: Psalms 23:1–4; 28:9; 74:1; 77:20; 78:52; 79:13; 80:1; 95:7; 100:3; Isaiah 40:11; 63:11; Jeremiah 13:17; 23:1–3; 50:6; Ezekiel 34:6, 8, 31; Micah 7:14. Achtemeier uses "tradition" in the sense of beliefs handed down orally until written.

28. Calvin, *Calvin's Commentaries,* 22:146.

CHAPTER 7: THINKING ABOUT TRANSITION TO ELDER LEADERSHIP

1. John Piper, "Elders, Bishops, and Bethlehem," a sermon at the Bethlehem Baptist Church, Minneapolis, MN, March 1, 1987 www.soundofgrace.com/piper87/jp870012.htm, page 7. (accessed Nov. 21, 2002).
2. For additional considerations on the problems of pragmatism, see my essay, "The Pastor and Church Growth: How to Deal with the Modern Problem of Pragmatism," in *Reforming Pastoral Ministry: Challenges for Ministry in Postmodern Times,* ed. John Armstrong (Wheaton, Ill.: Crossway, 2001), 263–80.
3. Jeff Noblit, Pastor-Teacher, First Baptist Church, Muscle Shoals, Alabama, telephone conversation, April 3, 2003.
4. Matt Schmucker, Director of the 9Marks Ministries, formerly the Center for Church Reform, 525 A Street NE, Washington, D.C. 20002, telephone conversation, April 3, 2003. 9Marks Ministries has a number of helpful resources on elders and church polity, as well as an extensive web site at www.9Marks.org.

CHAPTER 8: CAN IT BE DONE? MAKING THE TRANSITION TO ELDER LEADERSHIP

1. I found Gene Getz, *Sharpening the Focus of the Church* (Wheaton, Ill.: Victor, 1984), to be helpful in identifying many passages for study. Gene Getz, *Elders and Leaders: God's Plan for Leading the Church* (Chicago: Moody, 2003), identifies additional texts for study.
2. This is the most plausible method for beginning elder leadership in any type of missionary setting. Assuming that the congregation is young and not well-versed in Scripture, the missionary will need to evaluate carefully potential candidates for elder, and then invest much time in training them before turning the reigns of leadership over to the elders on behalf of the church. Maintaining contact with the elders to "coach" them through the early years of leadership could prove invaluable to the church's future.
3. Mark Dever, Senior Pastor of Capitol Hill Baptist Church, Washington, D.C., telephone conversation on February 3, 2004.

CHAPTER 9: PUTTING IT ALL TOGETHER

1. Leon Morris, *The First and Second Epistles to the Thessalonians,* rev. ed., The New International Commentary of the New Testament, (Grand Rapids: Eerdmans, 1991), 167.

2. Ray Steadman, quoted by Jim Henry, "Pastoral Reflections on Baptist Polity in the Local Church," (address given at the "Issues in Baptist Polity Conference", New Orleans Baptist Theological Seminary, February 5, 2004).

3. Quotation from Paige Patterson in response to the author's question about how single pastoral authority lacks accountability, "Panel Discussion: Issues in Baptist Polity," New Orleans Baptist Theological Seminary, February 6, 2004.

4. John Hammett, personal dialogue, New Orleans, LA, February 6, 2004.

5. For more information on conference papers, see www.baptistcenter.com.

6. Mark Dever, "Baptist Elders: Contradictory, or Consistent?" www.9marks.org/partner/Article_Display_Page/0,,PTID314526|CHID598016|CIID1, page 15.

7. Donald MacLeod, "Presbyters and Preachers," Monthly Record of the Free Church of Scotland, June 1983, 124.

8. Gerald Cowen, Who Rules the Church? Examining Congregational Leadership and Church Government (Nashville: Broadman and Holman, 2003), 39.

9. Ibid., 82.

10. Ibid., 14.

11. Ibid., 14–16.

12. John Calvin, The Epistles of Paul to Timothy and Titus (1548–50; reprint, London: Oliver and Boyd, 1964), 263, quoted and expanded upon in John Stott, Guard the Truth: The Message of 1 Timothy and Titus (Downers Grove, Ill.: InterVarsity, 1996), 138.

13. R. Albert Mohler, "Church Discipline: The Missing Mark," in Polity: Biblical Arguments on How to Conduct Church Life, ed. Mark Dever (Washington, D.C.: Center for Church Reform, 2001), 53.

Select Bibliography

Ascol, Thomas K., ed. *Dear Timothy: Letters on Pastoral Ministry.* Cape Coral, Fla.: Founders Press, 2004.

Dever, Mark E. *A Display of God's Glory: Basics of Church Structure.* Washington, D.C.: Center for Church Reform, 2001.

———. "Baptist and Elders," originally delivered at the "Issues in Baptist Polity Conference", New Orleans, La., Feb. 6,2004. http://www.9marks.org/partner/Article_Display_Page/0,,PTID314526|CHID626244|CIID1744980,00.html.

———. *Nine Marks of a Healthy Church.* Revised edition. 2000. Reprint, Wheaton, Ill.: Crossway, 2004.

———, ed. *Polity: Biblical Arguments on How to Conduct Church Life.* Washington, D.C.: Center for Church Reform, 2001.

———. "Should a Church Have Elders?" http://www.9marks.org/CC/article/0,,PTID314526|CHID598016|CHID1643290,00.html.

———. "What is the Relationship Between the Elders and the Church?" http://www.9marks.org/partner/Article_Display_Page/0,,PTID314526|CHID626244|CIID1552942,00.html.

Getz, Gene. *Elders and Leaders: God's Plan for Leading the Church—A Biblical, Historical and Cultural Perspective.* Chicago: Moody, 2003.

MacArthur, John, Jr., ed. *Rediscovering Pastoral Ministry: Shaping Contemporary Ministry with Biblical Mandates.* Dallas: Word, 1995.

———. *The Master's Plan for the Church.* Chicago: Moody, 1991.

Merkle, Benjamin. "Hierarchy in the Church." http://www.9marks.org/CC/article/0,,PTID314526|CHID598016|CIID1710880,00.html.

Newton, Phil A., "The First Steps in Changing Church Leadership Structure." http://www.9marks.org/CC/article/0,,PTID314526|CHID598016|CIID1826822,00.html.

Piper, John. *Biblical Eldership: Shepherd the Flock of God Among You.* http://www.DesiringGod.org/library/tbi/bib_eldership.html

———. *Biblical Eldership.* Minneapolis: Desiring God Ministries, 1999.

Ryken, Philip. *City on a Hill: Reclaiming the Biblical Pattern for the Church in the Twenty-first Century.* Chicago: Moody, 2003.

Strauch, Alexander. *Biblical Eldership: An Urgent Call to Restore Biblical Church Leadership.* Revised and expanded. Littleton, Colo.: Lewis and Roth Publishers, 1995.

Wills, Gregory. *Democratic Religion: Freedom, Authority, and Church Discipline in the Baptist South, 1785–1900.* New York: Oxford University Press, 1997.

Scripture Index

Subject Index